# Lighting the Mosquito Coast

Irishman John Ruddock's Half-Century
Adventure, Raw Faith and Results
Pioneering in the Jungle
for the Lord

*An oral autobiography
told to Barry Colman*

Christian Missions in Many Lands
P.O. Box 13, Spring Lake, N.J. 07762

# Dedication

This book is dedicated to Margaret Randall and my mother Johnette Colman. They sacrificed for the Lord's work in Honduras, even as infants. It is also for all those who supported John's and Nettie's work for the Lord. And especially for the pioneering missionaries-to-be.

In appreciation to Betty Lukas for encouragement and long hours editing and proofing; to Todd Mindermann for creating the cover; to Karen Proctor for the proofreading and the clean, efficient typing; and to Harriet Ducott for painstakingly getting it all transcribed from tape.

And thanks to Maria for her understanding and love; to Natalie for listening to the stories every other night; and to Lukas for the goos and gahs.

# Contents

# Contents

# Foreword

*I am the light of the world; he that followeth me shall not walk in darkness, but shall have the light of life.*                    John 8:12

*I am come a light into the world, that whosoever believeth on me shall not abide in darkness.*                    John 12:46

*There was a man sent from God, whose name was John. The same came for a witness, to bear witness of the Light, that all men through him might believe. He was not that Light, but was sent to bear witness of that Light. That was the true Light, which lighteth every man that cometh into the world.*                    John 1:6-9

This book is written in my grandfather's own words, as if you are sitting in a room listening to him intimately recall his life. I taped many hours of conversation with him remembering his 52 years in Central America. I traveled to Ireland with him and revisited the places of his child- and young adult-hood and recorded more.

I then edited those words to flow like a long-anticipated, cherished personal letter. This oral book format captures his driven but contagiously happy personality. He usually had a glint in his eyes, like a little boy awaiting the culmination of a prank. He was known to pull a few, as you'll find out later in the book.

He also wore a subtle smile and was animated in conversation, using his arms for punctuation and his face for emotions. He was small yet energetic, almost nervous, but warm and accessible. His way with words comes through here in this oral history. The book also contains several letters written by him in the 1930s and '40s from Honduras. The sparkle of his personality shows in the words. When I was young, he would periodically show up at our home in Los Angeles in a mud-encrusted four-wheel drive Jeep or on a Pan Am jet. He would bring leopard and wild pig skins, sawfish saws and three-foot long machete swords. He would also bring stories of the Honduran bush and native Indians that brought the jungle to life in my imagination-prone mind.

You only had to listen to him utter any few words or watch him interact with a waitress or grocery store clerk to know he was on a mission from which no person, thing or place could distract him. He was first and foremost a single-minded servant of the Lord.

But he enjoyed every minute of it – in a contagious way. In any setting, he could break the ice with a joke, a prank or simply an unexpected question. He was energized with the spark and curiosity of a child for his entire life. He would bet me that I couldn't stay awake all night, and mean it. He would instruct me to say "when" as he poured milk and then overflow the glass if I didn't. But most important, he showed me that being a Christian didn't have to be boring. It could be fun to serve the Lord.

In Honduras, he would efficiently lay out his clothes every evening to allow him to literally jump into his pants and shoes while buttoning his shirt on the way out the door. He couldn't bear to waste a minute of the Lord's time. That story, better than any of the hundreds of others, captures what John Ruddock's life was all about: enthusiasm for the Lord. He came closer to anyone I've known, or I may ever know, to seeing the world through the Lord's eyes.

I think you will feel you know him before you read very far. I think you will like him and his stories of adventure for the Lord. Much of the book, in fact, reads like a fictional adventure. He was a very effective storyteller for he had many years of practice. Listen for his mixed Irish and Spanish-language accent as you read. Yes, he led a life of high adventure, but that wasn't what was important to him and he certainly didn't go looking for it. In fact, the only thing that was important to him was sharing the light of Christ. I received a telling phone call from him late in his life.

The phone rang twice and then clicked mid-ring to the answering machine. I ran late to grab it, but my grandfather spoke into the receiver at Western Assemblies Missionary Home in Claremont, California. "I have light," he said. "The battery works boy. I have light."

I cried this day in June, 1987 as I remembered the verses about the light of Christ, his story of the first lights in Newcastle, and all those years he had devoted to lighting darkened lives in Central America. This 89-year-old man had given his life to the Light of the World and it was still shining through him. He was obsessed with it, and had devoted his life to lighting the world with it

As a boy, he had dreamed of creating a battery that drew on sea water for electrical current to power clocks and lights and inventing a perpetual motion machine, but, much like everything else in his life, he had put those temporal things aside to concentrate on something infinitely more powerful. Now, in his old age, he was experimenting with the battery again.

He had often contrasted his life with a schoolmate and boyhood friend in his Irish homeland who chose the other path, one that was out of the light. Chum Harry Ferguson, who experimented with the first flying machines in Ireland, then turned his inventive talent to tractor design, had become wealthy. Even though he was respected throughout the world, he died an embittered man as described in *Harry Ferguson: Inventor and Pioneer* by Colin Fraser.

It was from that bitter darkness that John Ruddock devoted his life to bringing salvation to the world, but before John Ruddock discovered the true light, he experimented with Thomas Edison's world-changing imitation.

As a young man, I planned to bring his stories to readers in the hope they would change lives for the better. He certainly changed many lives while he walked the earth, mine included. Now I trust you will not only be entertained but also inspired by his words. Meet John Ruddock, as he helps turn on the first lights in Newcastle, Ireland.

* * *

In Newcastle, we were very busy, practically working night and day. Everything had to be done, from the building of the power house itself to the installation of engines, dynamos, and the switchboard, as well as the street lighting. At last, all was in order. The engines were working, the dynamos were humming, and everything was performing as it should. Then came the day when the lights were to be turned on for the first time.

We had already fixed up a special platform in the promenade in the center of town. Special seating was arranged in the open air in the front of this platform for spectators. Fortunately, there was no rain. A fellow worker, John Shannon, was there supervising everything. I was in the power house. My ears, well accustomed to the noise of the engines and the low hum of the dynamos, listened for that which I did not want to hear: trouble.

My eyes stayed glued to the instruments and indicators on the switchboard, and the clock. I eagerly waited for the signal from partner John to throw the main switch that would turn on the lights. The count down, according to the clock, was down to 5 seconds, then 4, 3, 2, 1. In came the signal from John and, at that second I threw the switch. The same moment, the mayor of the town, standing on the platform in the promenade, flipped on his switch for all the spectators to see, and on went the lights for the first time ever in Newcastle, Ireland. He got a great cheer from the crowd. Everyone thought he had turned them on when, of course, I had, and I got nothing.

Thinking on this experience many times in later life, I have been greatly encouraged by the fact that there is One above who is always at the controls, keeping everything in order. Down here on earth, there is seemingly much work; everyone is busy doing this, that, and the other thing, but up above is where the real control is.

I have also experienced comfort and help while laboring all alone by the fact that I may be doing a bigger, greater, and more important work than I did that day in Newcastle when I switched on the lights for the first time.

# Introduction

*Dear Young Believer in the Lord Jesus Christ:*

*Thank the Lord, somehow, somewhere, Man's ruin was brought to your attention. You learned that you were a guilty sinner on your way to receive punishment for your sins in eternity. God's remedy was also brought to your attention through perhaps John 3:16. God's only Son took your guilty place, receiving the punishment for you.*

*Then your responsibility was pressed upon you; your belief or faith in Him and the work He did for you, resting entirely on Him. You did nothing, nothing in the common sense of the word but, yes, you did what He asked you to do: believe in the Lord Jesus Christ. This you did and now you are saved.*

*You have also obeyed Him in baptism, burying the old man and rising again to live a new life. On the first day of the week you meet regularly to remember Him as He requested along with the two or three who gather together in His name. Wonderful. Thank the Lord.*

*As you read His word daily, and speak to Him in prayer, you may find He is calling you to dedicate your life to do a special work for Him. In my case it was to go to a far off land and take the Good News of Salvation to those who live there.*

*Perhaps you think He is calling you. Let me inject a word of warning here. Take time and make sure He is calling you. He may not call you in the same way as I was called but He will in some way make it clear to you that you are to go. This is important. If He calls and sends you, everything else will be taken care of; material, financial, yes, everything.*

*My wife and I can testify to that. During our 52 years in the mission field, the Lord supplied all that was necessary. It was never necessary to beg. If He wanted us to do a certain thing, He always supplied the means to do it, and He can do the same for you if He sends you.*

*In days gone by, I have been told that I should record a book and, later, I found myself in a position that I could not resist. I speak it with the prayer that it may be useful and used by the Lord to help other pioneer missionaries like myself.*

# CHAPTER 1: Four Birthdays

Trujillo, Republica de Honduras
Central America
18th May 1936

My wife was born in Kilwinning, Ayrshire, Scotland, on the 25th May 1901. She was born again in Saltcoats, Scotland, on the 5th March 1918. After her conversion, she was especially interested in missionary work in Roman Catholic countries. Through hearing a missionary from one of these countries speak at a conference in Paisley, Scotland, she became definitely exercised about serving the Lord in South America. The speaker spoke about the great need for workers and brought before the young especially the first verse of Romans 12. This message stayed with her.

Later she left Scotland and went to the United States, finally settling in Pasadena, California. She was in fellowship in Jefferson Street Assembly, Los Angeles. On the way from Pasadena to Los Angeles, the streetcar passed through a part of the Mexican district. She noticed the people and learned that they were Mexicans. She asked the sister in the Lord with whom she traveled if anything was being done for these Mexicans, and in this way learned about the work which I had commenced among them. In Pasadena, she lived next door to Miss Ulrich, (a sister who was responsible for sending *Mensajes de Amor* to the many Spanish-speaking countries) and from her she heard more about the Mexicans. It was in Miss Ulrich's home that my wife and I first really became acquainted. Along with another sister, Miss Storrie, she began helping me in the Mexican district. Later we became engaged to be married, and a year later we were married in Pasadena.

. . . .

I was born in Growell, Dromore, County Down, Ireland on the 17th December 1897. I was born again on the 26th September 1918, in the town of Newry, Ireland.

After my conversion, the foreign field and its need were constantly before me, but I am afraid I was not willing to hear God's voice speak to me. Along with another brother in Christ, who is now laboring in Africa, I spent most of my spare time in distributing tracts and joining in open-air meetings.

Some time after this, along with my family, I left Ireland and came to reside in Los Angeles, California. It was not long before I saw the need for the gospel among the Mexicans of that city. Asking God to help me, I began to work among the Mexican children in my spare time. Renting a house in which to hold meetings, I went around to some of the homes with gospels and tracts, and invited the children to the meetings. Soon quite a number of children were coming regularly, and some of the older folks began to come, too. God blessed the effort with the result that some were saved, and the brother who still carries on that work in Los Angeles tells me that God continues to bless by saving souls. All this time I was exercised about the work further afield and hoped that one day the way would be opened up for me to go to serve the Lord in Mexico.

That country, however, was closed to missionaries and so the door was closed to me. It was at this time that I met my wife. She, too, was interested in the Spanish-speaking peoples, and had been exercised about serving the Lord in South America. We became engaged to be married and definitely put the matter of our future life service before the Lord, desiring only to be led by Him.

Shortly after this a letter came to me from Brother Kramer in Guatemala telling about the need there. This caused us to seriously consider the matter of serving the Lord in Guatemala, and so we made it a definite matter of prayer. After waiting on the Lord, we laid it before the elders of our assembly. They, after prayerful consideration, commended us to the work of the Lord, and in October of 1926 we left Los Angeles for Quetzaltenango, Guatemala. This was our first station.

When Brother Kramer returned from furlough, we all felt it would be more advantageous to the work if we went to live on the coast of Guatemala in the town of San Felipe. So, after having been two years in Quetzaltenango, we went to San Felipe and, after two years service there, returned to the British homeland on account of my health.

On our return from furlough we came to San Pedro Sula, Honduras, to Mr. Hockings. While in Guatemala we had heard from him of the great need in Honduras. After visiting many parts of this republic, we felt led to stay as the need was indeed great. In this State of Colon, where we live, there is no other missionary from any of the sects or missions. There are thousands of Caribs who have never heard the gospel, besides the Spanish-speaking people, and in the Mosquito District, there are Indians, too, who have not yet heard the story of God's free gift.

We have two children, Margaret Jean, age six years and seven months, and Cornelia Johnette, age two years and three months.

. . . .

From the 1936 Annual Report of the National Bible Society of Scotland: "Honduras is one of the most needy of the Central American Republics. Politically, the country is always seething with unrest, while a lack of roads and railways to connect up a sparse population scattered over a mountainous country of 46,000 square miles makes missionary work a difficult task. The workers are few, widely separated, and the whole environment is unsympathetic toward a religious life."

# CHAPTER 2: The First Born and Most Mischievous Son

Growell, Dromore, County Down in Ireland, where I was born is a very famous part of the country. I went to a little school there along with the neighbor children. One of them happened to be the famous Harry Ferguson, of tractor fame. He was a little older than I was. I knew his brothers very well. There was quite a number of them. They were our playmates. We also went to Sunday school together in the gospel hall which was nearby. Harry went to Sunday school. His father was a Christian. In fact, he was the one that gave the ground, first of all, for the gospel hall to be built. It was an old stable that they had kept horses in, but it was out of use at the time. He handed it over as a gospel hall. My grandfather was the first to form a Sunday school there. He carried that Sunday school on for many years. My father was a gospel preacher; he would travel out to the country places and hold gospel meetings in tents, barns, kitchens, any place he could find open to proclaim the gospel. I was brought up in a Christian home under the influence of a Christian mother, which indeed I am very thankful for. There were evil influences, of course, that might have carried me in other directions had I not had that foundation.

Harry was quite an engineer from the day of his birth. He later built the first airplane in Ireland. He also flew that plane. He spent some considerable time trying to get the plane to fly. Even later, he made a famous flight in Newcastle where he fell, broke his nose and wrecked the plane. I don't think he did very

4

much flying after that. Harry's brother was older and had an auto agency in Belfast, so Harry went along with his brother in the auto business. At the same time, he was very much interested in all kinds of engineering, especially agricultural engineering. That was about the time that tractors were coming in; however, they were not quite a success in many ways. While hauling a plow behind them, if the plow contacted a big stone, the tractor would rear up like a horse and sometimes fall over backwards killing the driver. Harry thought he could improve upon that, which he eventually did.

He spent some time on his father's farm near where we lived plowing with a horse. He intentionally hit stones to feel their effect on the handles. When he got an idea, he left the horses and ran off to Belfast to work on his tractor design. I saw him plowing that day in the field in front of our own home. I asked Ted, his brother, what Harry was doing. He told me he was plowing to figure out the real reason tractors reared up. He spent several years trying and re-trying his design until at last he perfected what he called the three-point system which you can find in every tractor today. They spent some time perfecting it and marketing it. He became very famous and made lots of money. You'll find the Ferguson tractor all over the world today.

That was the environment in which I grew up. I, too, must have been born an engineer. I remember the first clock I repaired. I was very successful in making that clock work again. Afterward, I was told that I was three years of age when I showed an interest in that sort of thing. I had lots of fun with clocks. I repaired any kind I could get my hands on. Some of them took considerable time and patience, and lots of thought. I would get one started and go to bed, but would not sleep. I would come down in the dark and listen to hear if the clock was ticking. If it wasn't ticking, I couldn't wait until morning; I wanted to know what time the clock stopped. There were no electric lights at that time, nothing but candles; however, I did not want to wake up the family. I would get up in a chair and try to feel where the hands of the clock were. Then I would know what time it had stopped. I would try to start the clock again in the dark. Sometimes I succeeded, sometimes I didn't. One night, I got up in the chair and one hand caught a bucket of coals used for lighting fires. I slipped, and down came the bucket of coals, and down went the chair. What an awful racket. I beat it back to bed as fast as I could. Pretty soon I heard my father come out and look around with a candle. He went back to bed and I heard him say to my mother, "Oh, it was only John. At his work as usual." However, I succeeded in repairing many other old clocks.

I remember working on that first clock at three years old. The last clock I worked on my age was 89 years. This was an electric clock, which ran on a small battery. However, after much thought and work, I succeeded in getting it to run on electricity made from sea water. It kept good time for months. It may have been the first and only clock to run on sea water.

As time went on, I went to school like everyone else. I had lots of fun those years. Thank the Lord for my mother and father, even though my father was out for most of the time, preaching the gospel in various places. My father was also very weak in many ways. Once he called me to his bedside; he was sure he was dying. He asked me to promise that I'd be a good boy and help my mother all I could. Being the eldest of the family, I bore a responsibility in helping my brothers and sisters. I had two sisters and three brothers. That made six of us all together. I never forgot that scene. He exhorted me also about eternal things and what I ought to do. At that time, things were very much different than today. Saturdays, we had a little work to do helping with the household duties and cleaning things up, but on Sunday all the pencils, paper, and school books were put to one side. All the balls, marbles, and other toys were put away, too. Sunday was a special day. We went to Sunday school in the morning. When we came home, we changed out of our Sunday-go-to-meeting clothes, put on our ordinary clothes, and got to work. Work wasn't the same on Sundays as on any other day. It meant we got out the Bible and started to learn scripture verses. At the next Sunday school we were supposed to repeat what we had learned during the previous week. I found in later years that to be a very good and necessary education. I spent some time learning ten verses every Sunday. I would repeat those ten verses the next Sunday in Sunday school. I learned to repeat the first ten chapters of Romans, Psalm 119, Psalm 23 and the first eight chapters of John. There were many other verses I could repeat by heart at any time without missing one word. I found in later years that was very useful indeed. My brother could learn them much faster than I could. I had to spend much time in repeating, reading and re-reading before I could remember those verses. Then there were also regular meetings.

My father would preach in a gospel tent along with some others. All through the years, wet or cold in any shelter he could find, he would preach. Meetings were going on constantly so I was occupied most of my free time when not at school by attending meetings. Sometimes I did not listen very well, but I did learn that I was a sinner. I learned that although I was born into a Christian home; although I went to Sunday school; although I could repeat verses; although I was raised to be a good boy; I was still a sinner. I needed the Savior. Eventually I found that Savior and put my trust and confidence in him, only then did I know that I was ready for eternity. All my sins had been forgiven and heaven was my home. As I learned more and more from the scriptures, I knew that the Lord Jesus Christ was soon coming to take all those that were His out of this world of sin and sorrow to be with Himself in Glory; however, years passed by before I had that real experience in my life.

In the meantime, I enjoyed myself to the fullest. At that time, there was not much opportunity to get into any kind of evil doings. We were brought up rather strictly and kept by ourselves quite a lot. We were not allowed to have much contact with many of the other children who had the liberty to do as they liked. I helped out quite a lot at home. My grandfather, living with us at that time, was a wonderful help to me. He was like myself, a little mechanically inclined. He was a constructor by trade. He built and repaired houses. Also, anyone that had machinery – and very few did at that time – would call on him to repair their machines. Some had combination threshers for corn and wheat, for example. I went along with him on such occasions and that gave me quite an education. I helped him in various ways. He would get up in the morning at 5:00. I would get up, too. He would go out to the garden and cultivate good eating potatoes and all kinds of vegetables: cabbage, carrots, parsnips, onions, leeks, celery and even quite a variety of berries.

We lived in a place where the hunt came around once in a while. Those with the time, money and the know-how spent much time hunting deer for fun. They'd bring the cart with a deer in it to a certain point, open the door and let the deer out. They'd wait for about a half an hour and then they'd let loose some 26 hounds. After they'd gotten the scent, away they would go. The huntsman with the red coat was supposed to follow them wherever they went. Behind him came many of the leisure-class people on good horses, both men and women. They would follow the huntsman and the hounds along the paths. They'd jump over the fences and cross the fields, wherever the deer would take them. On such times, we were allowed out of school. We, too, were quite interested. There was a special prize for those who could catch the deer, and that was a rather diffi-cult thing to do. The deer were very swift and would run for miles and miles with the dogs in hot pursuit. The hounds were very good in chasing the scent.

Once I remember the deer crossing through the grounds where we lived. The deer jumped the gate, went up the fence to another field and away he disappeared. Pretty soon the hunts-man was behind the dogs near the deer along with all the others behind. After some little time, the deer came back from another direction. It came down again, crossed his path through our land and went into a little lake at the back of the house. The huntsman couldn't cross the water with the horse and the deer was in the water. He gave me the horse to hold, which meant two shillings or a half a crown for me. He got in a little boat, went out and got the deer off the little island onto which it had escaped. The huntsman got back on his horse and took off again after the deer. All the other huntsmen and ladies followed him. I believe they lost that deer. That deer was too smart for them.

I spent my spare time in many things. Once I made an air-plane. I don't mean a toy; I mean one that you're supposed to fly in. I put wings on it and got my brothers to push me off a cliff. I flapped the wings, but down I came with a thump. It wouldn't fly. I copied other machines. I made a horse and cart. I made a potato digger. I also flew kites and put lanterns on them with a candle. They were a weird sight at night, with the light bouncing all over the sky. There were many other things we did. We played marbles and played ball. We trundled hoops, a round piece of iron with a hook on it. We had quite some races with those. I helped on the little farm that we had. We just grew the necessities of life on it. We had wonderful times down at the lake which bordered our ground. We had just a little piece of land, not very much, but it had a very comfortable house on it, and lots of room to play, which suited us children.

The house was made of stone and it had a nice little porch on the front which had a thatched roof on part of it. A thatched roof was the mode in those days. One thing about a thatched roof is that it made the house warm. Although it might be cold outside, it was quite warm inside because of the thatched roof. Another part of the house that had been added on had a slate roof. That part of the house was called the parlor in those days. That's where you took all guests that came along to visit you. None of us children were supposed to get in there. It was closed up until visitors came. Above that parlor was a loft. That was my quarters, where I slept, repaired the clocks, and studied. It was my own. There was a very narrow stair up to it which was rather difficult to get up, but it was a good thing for me because it kept all the other people out. I was very happy up there all alone, working.

As the eldest, I was supposed to have more sense than the rest. I don't know whether I did or not, but I know one thing: we were all up to some kind of tricks. I teased my sisters quite a bit; however, I think at heart they enjoyed it. We all went to school together. My brother was a year younger, but he took the lead in class. His name was Hugh. I never did like to be at the head of the class, and I found that was to be my trait ever since. I never tried to get first, but I was pretty careful not to be last. The teacher told me I would never be able to sing and I'd never be able to write properly. Regarding writing, he was wrong. Although I'm 80 years of age, I'm told by others that they can very easily read my writing. I always tried to write in such a way that others could read it. As for singing, he was right. I never was able to sing, but mental arithmetic came easy to me.

We played at home, in fact everything was a family affair at that time. The farm was rather small. It could hardly even be called a farm. It was more like a home and garden. We consumed the vegetables I helped my grandfather grow. We always had two cows for milk. In those days, you made your own butter. After the milk was collected in a crock for about a week, then it was emptied into a churn. We had to churn for almost an hour before the butter appeared. My mother then took over, emptied the butter out and prepared it. Of course, she also looked after the food. She could prepare good food. My mother's name was Margaret. Her maiden name was Margaret McCracken. My father's name was Andrew Ruddock. In those days, we didn't use Margaret or Andrew. It was always Mr. and Mrs. That was the way everyone addressed them, especially younger people. Those were the days also when children were supposed to be seen and not heard; however, we made ourselves heard at times when the coast was clear. When visitors came, then there was silence. Once the visitors left, we had free liberty to exercise the strength of our lungs. Which, indeed, we did with gusto. We spent a very happy time there.

We lived in a place where there were few people. Looking out our door, a little to the left lived the Shannon family. They were our nearest neighbors. Many times I was allowed to go up and

visit them. There was a boy about my own age, Willie. I spent
lots of time with him. They had a big farm, lots of cows and
horses and pigs and hens. I was very happy to help Willie do
his chores. He had to look after the cows or slice turnips. He
had a machine to do that. I would get the handle of the wheel to
make it go around and the turnips would be sliced according to
what was needed. He also looked after the horses. I never did
care much about horses so I kept my distance there. They also
had a pump in the yard that pumped water out of the well for
use in the house.

In those days, as well as the parlor, there was a big kitchen.
The kitchen was the place where much work was done. There
was an open fire that burned coal. It was necessary to blow on
the fire to keep it burning hot. Hand bellows were used for that.
Many times I sat blowing up the fire. A big pot of potatoes
might be boiling over the fire. They'd be a special kind. If they
were for the pigs or the hens, we used another kind of potato.
Many times I sat at the Shannon's eating dinner. The man of the
house, Willie's father James, was quite a jolly old lad. He kept
us laughing and in fun. Every time the potato plate would be almost empty, he would shout, "Is there no potatoes in this
house?" Then some of the girls would get up and bring more
potatoes. He gave us a good example in eating. In fact, he told
us that there was a hole in his stomach, and as soon as he'd eat
the potatoes, they would fall through this hole. That's the only
explanation he could give for eating so much. We had wonderful
times up there. He had more sons. There was John, John was
quite a grown man. He was an electrician out working in the cities and other places. His brother Robert was also an electrician.
They were much older than Willie and me. One night at eleven
o'clock while I was almost asleep, a knock came to the door. It
was to tell us that Robert Shannon had been electrocuted in
Dublin. That caught my attention right away. At that time, I did
not know much about electricity, but I understood that it was a
very dangerous thing. When I heard, I said to myself: "Why
don't you get busy and take the dangerous part out of electricity?" I remember that, unaware that in years to come I'd be very
much occupied with electricity.

The Fergusons lived to the right of us. Harry Ferguson had
brothers a little younger than himself that we ran about with. We
went to school with them; however, we were not allowed to stay
very long in their presence as they were supposed to be rather
wild and got into trouble many times. We were taught to keep

away from trouble so we were not permitted to be much in their company; however, sometimes that could not be avoided. When we got together, there was always some fun. During potato season, we young boys would help the farmers around us. We did it more for fun then for pay, but we were well paid. We'd make a fire, and put a few potatoes on it to roast out in the field. Many times, we would sit down for a rest after work and eat those roasted potatoes without salt, without butter and without a knife or fork. On one occasion, when we had finished the days work, one of Harry's brothers, Ted, said to me, "Let us frighten Freddie tonight." Freddie was a cousin of mine. It was Freddie's duty to take the cows home from the field. This night when he went to get the cows, Ted took off his coat and turned it inside out. The lining was all white so he was going to be a ghost that night. He hid behind the hedge until the cows passed and Freddie got alongside and then he made an awful noise and gave his arms a flutter. It was rather dark and Freddie could see nothing but white, and he supposed it was a ghost. Poor Freddie was frightened and ran for his life, yelling, "The ghost is after me. The ghost is after me." He ran as fast as he could, jumped over a hedge and through a field to home. His mother came out thinking someone was murdered, but Freddie kept running right past her. He ran into the kitchen and hid under the table, still certain the ghost was after him. By that time, Ted and I were on our way home. We were innocent, of course.

When I grew older and was working, I went to visit my cousins. I had a few living here and some there and some somewhere else, so it took me some time to visit them all. On this occasion, I visited Freddie's brother Ernie. When Ernie and I got together there was more fun still. The first night I got into bed, the bed started to walk all over the floor. It was Ernie underneath. He was big and strong. He'd gotten up on his hands and knees, and lifted the bed up with his back and ran across the floor with it. Well, that did not trouble me in the least. The next night, he was sure he was going to frighten me and make me run. He went away on an errand to a distant town. When he had to make that trip he would get up early and not get home until it was rather late. While he was away, I left that house, my aunt's, and went to visit another cousin. Ernie, of course, did not know this. In the meantime, a lady came to visit my aunt. She was quite a character, an old maid, and rather peculiar in her ways. She was a great walker, but very, very slow. Once I had to walk with her and it was agony because she walked so slow; however, she always got where she wanted to go. On this occasion, she wanted to come to my aunt's and, right enough, she got there rather late in the evening. My aunt put her into the bed that I had been using along with Ernie the night before. My aunt intended to sit up and tell Ernie to take another room when he got home later, but she went to sleep. When Ernie came home, he thought I was there just as the night before. This was the night that he was going to really frighten me. He slipped up the stairs, opened the door, very easily. He gave one spring and landed on what he thought was the top of me. Instead of it being me, of course, it was this old maid Arabella. And, my, when he jumped onto the top of her, there was a yell. "Murder, murder, murder." I don't know who was frightened more, Arabella or Ernie. After Ernie got his hands in her hair he didn't know what to think or what to do so he shouted, too. His mother came running in and, my, what a scene that was. Ernie soon got over it; however, the next morning Arabella had had enough of that house and away she went to another house. Soon my visiting was over, too.

After living in Growell, because of my father's poor health we moved to another place, Ballygorian near Rathfriland. Rathfriland was a rather peculiar town in many ways. It was built up on a hill. They called it Rathfriland-upon-the-hill. You had to climb up a steep road if you wanted to get to it from any place. It didn't matter from which direction you came. There was no train into Rathfriland. The train came to Ballyroney. When you got to Ballyroney, you got off the train. At Ballyroney there was a gentleman by the name of Larry Downey. He had an Irish jaunting car, and he would be right pleased and happy to take you any place you wished to go. Of course, it was his business, and that's the way he made his living.

The jaunting car, by the way, was quite a car. There were two seats on each side of the car that faced outward. Each side held two passengers. You sat up on the side looking out, with no protection. Between the two seats there was a special well for the passengers' luggage. The driver sat up on the top and directed the horse that pulled the car. One day, I was going to Hillsboro and it was a rather frosty morning. The horse was slipping all over the place. Once he went right down onto his knees, and when he went down, I fell right off the car. I didn't hurt myself. I just picked myself up, got onto the Irish jaunting car, and away we went again. They also had at that time something called horses and traps. With the trap you sat inside instead of outside. Many people owned traps for going short distances. That was the mode of travel in those days in Ireland. That was before the days of the car, the auto, or even the motorcycle. So any time that you wanted to go from Ballyroney station to Rathfriland, Larry Downey would take you up in the jaunting car. The man who swept the streets was kind of a poet, and so was Larry Downey. Larry Downey and he set up some entertainment for the passengers. When this man was sweeping the streets, Larry would come up with his jaunting car and the sweep would say to him, "Down to Ballyroney, it is not very far, but here comes Larry Downey with his jaunting car." And then Larry would say to him, "You silly loon, lift up your broom, and let a body by." And the sweep would say to Larry, "You silly loon, you have room to pass between the wall and I."

Once in a while we'd go to Rathfriland to get provisions, and we walked. It was about three-quarters-of-an-hour's walk, more or less. It was a very pleasant walk with nice scenery, but the trouble was getting up the hill. You'd puff your lungs all the way up that hill walking; however, over time, I owned one of those motorcycles. It was a Rudgemulty. That was the name. A Rudgemulty was a cycle that had variable gears on it. It was kind of automatic, so when you came to a hill or high place on the road, automatically, it went into another gear. You could also control the gears by your hand. It was a glorified bicycle, you might say.

After about six years, we came back to our old home in Growell. I was growing up a little bigger, but I don't know whether I had any more sense than when I was young; however, I did have more responsibilities. I had to help fix up the house. It had been vacant for a while and needed repairs so I helped my father repair it. At one time, there had been a bakery at that house. There was a lean-to built onto one of its sides. This lean-to had been used when I was a small boy to stable a pony that my father used sometimes on his travels. Now it was in bad repair, and also, the gable, as they called it, was in bad repair. So much so that part of it at least had to be torn down. My uncle, who was very expert in such things, started to work on it. He took the old stable down altogether, cleared the stones away and started on the gable. He was up a ladder working when old Joe Ruddock came along. Now, old Joe was a brother of my grandfather's. He was an old, old man, but still very much alive. He maintained that there was a treasure buried somewhere near and he believed it was in that part of the house. He sat down beginning to think where it could be. My uncle got into the act and asked us to lend him our ball. In those days, we did not have the luxury of owning a rubber ball, it was one we made ourselves. We wrapped up brown paper, tied it with cord, wrapped more paper, tied it with cord, wrapped it with old cloth and tied it with cord and kept that up until we had a good football. My uncle got a hold of that ball. He took it up the ladder with him. After working for a few minutes he shouted. "Hello, hello," and he threw down the ball. "There it is," he said. And then he cried, "Oh, what did I throw the treasure away for?" He tried to come down the ladder very quickly but old Joe ran and got a hold of the ball, and do you think anyone could get it from him? No sir. He held onto that ball and he began to untie it. Us boys were all standing bursting to laugh, and could barely keep our faces straight. Old Joe tried to get the cords unloose. He hollered at my uncle to help him. He kept at it and kept at it. My uncle encouraged him by saying, "Oh, it must be in there. It must the next layer." The poor old man spent all afternoon unraveling that ball, thinking it was a treasure. How sad he was when he came to the last cord, unraveled the last piece of paper and found nothing. My uncle could hardly keep from laughing. It was quite a joke for a long time to come. Now we had to start in and make a new ball for ourselves.

But June was the month of the year for us children. School was off for three weeks. Off we'd go to our Grandmother's (Mother's mother) in Mullertown, beyond Newcastle near Annalong. Mullertown was a big farming community, near the sea. It was part of the Mourne district where the mountains of Mourne sweep down to the sea. On the way there you passed Maggie's Leap, which was a very deep, wide hole. Maggie was supposed to have jumped over it when chased by a mad bull. The Windy Gap was also a place of interest. There, you hold on to your hat.

To get there we walked to Dromore, then took the train to Newcastle. In Newcastle, Old Arthur was waiting with his Long Car. The Long Car was really a double jaunting car with four wheels drawn by two horses or a vehicle called the Mourne Mountain. A ladder was needed to get into it but once in it you had a good view. We all enjoyed Mullertown. There was so much to see and we had a wonderful time with our cousins. Then we returned home.

As my father was away, I took charge of planting potatoes

and vegetables. I looked after the cows and helped my mother with the hens. I helped her churn the butter and make buttermilk. After the churning, a big white sheet was put outside on a certain bush. When the neighbors saw that, they knew that there was buttermilk to come buy. Eventually, I finished my education there and began to make my own way as a man.

# CHAPTER 3: Two Lives Saved; From a Wall and a Well

While I was attending school as a boy, we had a half hour walk to the school house. There was lots to see and lots to do on the way. One day, I saved an old man's life. There was a place along the road where people sat in the evenings. It was called a ditch. It was really a rock wall, but a nice place to sit. This old man had the habit of coming down and sitting there on cool afternoons. This day, when I was passing by, I looked over and all I could see were two feet. I went over and saw this old man lying there with his head down and his feet up. He was blue in the face. He couldn't move. He was very heavy so I couldn't pull him up, either. I looked around and saw a man coming on a cycle. I stopped him and said, "Old Jim is lying here. I'm afraid he can't get up." So this man, by the name of George Bell, got off the bike. He came over and said, "He's almost dead. Help me to get him up." We both pulled at the man and eventually we got him up, but the poor old soul still couldn't move. We had to practically carry him home which fortunately was not very far away. That old man owed his life to us.

As you know, things can come back to you at times in life. A time came in my own life when I was getting to be an old man that I was also rescued from such a fate. I got into a well from which I could not get out. I was drawing water from a well in Honduras and my glasses fell in. Without thinking of my age, condition or anything else, I took off my pants and boots and let myself into the well. I figured I could just put my hand down and grab my glasses which were floating in the water. Before letting myself right into it I thought I had better see if I could get

16

out. Do you think I could get out? No, I couldn't get out. There I was, unable to climb out and not wanting to lower myself any further into the deep water. I tried to get my toes in a place to pull myself up, but there was nothing solid. I scraped my toes until they bled. Then I tried my knees. The same thing. The blood was running out of my knees. I was beginning to get exhausted because all this time I was shouting. No one could hear me because it was a rather lonely place. At last I was able to get my head up out of the well, nothing more. I found a place where I could put my big toe. I put it into a hole to steady myself, but I could get no further. Finally, I realized that there was nothing for me to do but keep quiet and conserve my strength. As long as my head was above water, I was all right. I prayed someone, sometime, would pass by and then I could cry for help.

Pretty soon, two girls came along. They had a little baby with them. I shouted, "Please, can you help me?" I told them I couldn't get out. I asked them if they would please go over and speak to the folks in the house a little further on and tell them that I was in this well and couldn't get out. They said they would, and away they went. Soon they came back to tell me there was no one there. Then I said, "Do you see that other house? Tell them." They went over and told the man who was there. I knew him, and soon he came running over. Between him and the two girls, they were able to pull me out of the well. I thanked him very much for it, but still I didn't have my glasses. By that time, it was dark so I thought I'd wait until the morning to get the glasses. In the morning, I did what I should have done at first. I got a rake and, on the second try, up came my glasses.

# CHAPTER 4: A New Job and a Saved Soul

A message came from Belfast from a cousin saying there was an opening in an electrical firm. They would be pleased to have me come and join them, if I liked. Of course, I liked. So I left my family and I made my way to Belfast. To get to Belfast, I had to. walk to the train station at Hillsboro. When I got into the train, another gentleman was there. I had my belongings with me in a little package. He looked at me and asked me where I was going. I told him and he gave me very good advice. He told me to be as good as I could, to tend to business, do what I was told and very soon I would get along very easily. I started into work. First of all I learned something about the bookkeeping end of the business, which allowed me at the same time to learn the names of the various electrical parts. When the workmen would come in, I would supply them with what they wanted. The boss I had was a very pleasant man, too, under certain conditions, and I soon learned what those conditions were. The second day I was there he came in and said to me, "John, will you go out and see if you can find me a clay pipe?" He smoked a pipe, but the trouble was he'd forgotten his pipe that morning.

He told me, "If I can't get my smoke, I'm telling you, there's no living with me. You will have a very, very sad time if I can't get a smoke, so you'd better go out and see if you can find me a pipe somewhere, a clay pipe. I've got my good ones at home but a clay pipe will do me today. If you don't come back with it you'd better keep out of my way." I went out and got the man a pipe, brought it in, and how happy he was. He thanked me. He told me I was worth my salt, and he and I got along all right after that.

When he would send me on messages, he wouldn't believe

18

that I'd gotten back so quickly. "Where did you go?" I'd say, "Didn't you send me to such and such a place?" "Yes, but how come you're back so soon? Did you run all the way?" I found out afterwards that he wasn't used to good work. He was used to sending a boy out who would spend half a day on a simple errand. I got in his good books, and he liked me very much. As time went on, I had the privilege of attending the Belfast Technical School. I thoroughly enjoyed myself there. There were all kinds of electrical apparatus for experimenting. I was expanding and learned quite a lot there.

I had to be at work at eight in the morning. At that time, they hadn't forgotten old Mr. Edison. They followed Thomas Edison's line of teaching. The first thing Edison did with a new boy, was to ask him to sweep the dust off the floor. He had method in that. He wanted to see how that floor was swept by these new boys. By that, he could soon tell what confidence he could put in him. I had to sweep the floor for a few days, but that didn't last long. He saw that I would do it, and wanted to work, and that's all he needed.

The time came when the company was starting a new plant. They called it the Irish Town's Electric Light and Power Company. They were lighting up for the first time several towns. Up to that time, there had been only gas used. This electricity was something new. We were contracting to electrify those cities and my boss wanted me to go to Newcastle to work under, who do you think? John Shannon, our old neighbor when I was growing up. I got there and I found a place to live. We had some fun in that place, too. My friend John Shannon and I didn't work regular hours. We got up in the morning early, sometimes at 5:00, and we worked until eleven o'clock at night. There was just the two of us preparing things for the real work. Pretty soon, we got others to come in to help us.

During my stay there, my brothers and sisters finished their education in Newcastle and, they, along with my parents, moved to the city of Belfast. Soon I joined them there. I had the intention of continuing in the technical college, but I found the Lord had something else in mind for me. One of the elders in the assembly in which we were in fellowship was a real young man's man. Upon arriving there, he invited me to join him and a few other young men, including T. Ernest Wilson. I was invited to his home along with a few more. When we arrived, we had a time of prayer. After prayer, Mrs. Patterson, this dear man's wife gave us hot cups of tea with lots of nice little things to eat. After that, we went out and found a place in Sandy Row where we could preach the gospel in the open-air. Soon we were all engaged in that kind of work. We spent much time also attending football fields or race tracks, anywhere a company of people would be gathered. We had, of course, a good supply of ammunition with us: gospel tracts. As those dear people would leave the football field, or other place of amusement, we would distribute these tracts among them. On Saturdays, we also were busy. We went to various villages and towns around us to distribute gospel tracts. After passing out tracts, we generally had an open air meeting. Some of these places were out of the way, but that is where the Gospel had to be taken.

On one occasion, Ernie Wilson and I were alone. It was a very wet, stormy night. Very few people were out, but somehow we decided that we would preach the gospel at a certain place. We could only see one man in attendance. He had his overcoat tucked around his neck and was standing in the shelter of a public house. That was a place where drink was sold. After preaching there for some time that evening, with the rain pouring down, we went home and forgot all about it. Years afterward, perhaps 25 or 30, a man stopped Ernest on the road and asked him if he were Ernest Wilson. He said, "Yes." "Do you remember preaching the gospel one night along with another young man?" he asked. "Yes," Ernest said. "Do you remember a man standing there listening?" "Yes." "Well, I'm that man. I never forgot what you said that night until God saved me. Now I'm in fellowship in one of the assemblies here." Ernest told me this years afterward and, of course, it made our hearts joyful to think that in some little measure at least, God had used that effort that we put forth in our young days.

# CHAPTER 5: The First Lights and a Holiday

I lived in Newcastle for three years, and worked with the Irish Towns Electric Light and Power Company. We installed the electrical system. There was no electricity in the country at that time, and every little town was getting its own power station. That was our work. I was putting in the power stations. They used anthracite coal at that time to power what was called the suction producer gas engine. You worked the fan to blow it up and keep the fire red. The coals were enclosed in a big stove. There was a pipe from that to what we called the scrubber. It was filled with coke. The gas passing through that coke cleaned the gas. We also had a water system in the scrubber to cool the gas before it got to the engine. You had to start the engine in those days by hand. I was pretty expert in that. I got so that I could do it all myself.

Generally, it took two to start the engine; one to blow up the fire and one to start the engine. The suction stroke of the engine was like a pump. It pumped in the gas from the generator through the scrubber, where it was cleaned, then came on through the throttle. You opened the throttle to a certain position and then you pulled the belt on a wheel and that started the engine. You had to put a bucket of coal in the hopper every hour. The hopper was up above. You opened the top of it and put in the bucket of coal. Then you shook the hopper and pulled down on the handle which allowed the anthracite coal to fall down into the generator. I was about 17 or so.

In Newcastle, I helped with all kinds of electrical work, in-house and outside work. This day, the boss came to me and said something was wrong in Newry. "I don't think it's much," he said. "I believe you can fix it up pretty well. They can't get things to work. It's been a long time since you had a vacation (actually I never did in those days). You can go up there, take about three weeks, and see what's wrong." I went to Newry to a place he told me about called the Lodge. It was a place, let me see now, run by a Mrs. Bond. That's where he had stayed the time he was there. Mrs. Bond was very happy to give me a place to sleep and to make me some food. I remember she had other boarders, too. We all had our own rooms. Mrs. Bond's daughter was there, and she was nice and very kind to us. We had lots of fun there. I was still full of mischief in those days.

I would go home on weekends to visit my parents. I traveled on a bicycle and then later on I got the Rudgemulty motorcycle and used that. I did a lot of work on motorcycles. I'd buy an old motorcycle, fix it up and then sell it again to make myself a few extra pennies. I would leave the Lodge on a Saturday evening to go home. Before departing, I'd always leave a little bit of fun for those who were in the house. In the bedroom in which I was, I would take all the pictures off the wall. Then I would wrap them up in the bed clothing. Sometimes I would turn the bed around and I'd put the chairs upside down. Other times I would lean them against the door so they wouldn't be able to open it. I'd leave the place and away I'd go, but I can tell you, when I came back Monday morning, ha, I had to be very careful. I brought a little life into the place anyhow. I spent some good times with Mrs. Bond there. Circumstances were such that her health was giving out, and I had to look for another place, which I soon found.

And it was, let me see now, the Waverly, that's what it was called. There was a little bakery there, and a little restaurant. That suited me, all right, I was sure of something to eat. I slept on the third floor. Some of the bakery men, bakery girls and res-taurant people had rooms, too. There were quite a few of us and fun was never lacking. I had some of my work people come to help out when it was necessary. When they came, there was al-ways more fun. I remember one night, there were three of us boys in the one room. It was plenty big with plenty of beds. We heard something in the passageway outside the door. We lis-tened and we heard some of the girls say, "What's the matter, what's wrong?" The fact was, they had peppered our beds before we got into them, and they were listening to hear us sneeze. When we didn't sneeze, they couldn't make it out. The secret was that we had been working on the engine and the gas fumes had gotten into our lungs, which prevented the pepper from taking effect. We were immune to their trick; however, we didn't forget them. I rigged up a light above their bed. It was only a two volt flashlight bulb that I used. I ran the wires up to our room, up above them, and put it on a little simple battery. Every once in a while I would touch the wires and cause lightning in their room. At least they thought it was lightning. They had been making lots of noise before, but when the lightning began to flash, it began to get quieter. When we asked what was wrong they said there was lots of lightning tonight. After we got them well frightened with the lightning, we put the light on and kept the light on. That frightened them even more. They couldn't make out what it was. Soon they got onto the idea that it was one of our tricks, and then they weren't so much afraid, but then they got back at us.

We got up in the morning, pretty early, sometimes four-thirty or five, before they were up, and there was no light, no electricity yet in this house. The house was dark at this time of the morning. We came down the stairs and when we reached the kitchen there were two individuals standing there. They didn't move. I said, "Good morning." They never answered. Being young, we weren't very easily frightened. It didn't affect us in the least. We bid our silent visitors good morning and went on. Afterward, we found out that the girls had made two dummy-men and placed them in our path thinking they would frighten us, but they didn't. That was our private life there, when we were off work. When we were working, we were very earnest and solemn, but those pranks added to the spice of life.

This was during World War I, and the landlady's husband had a brother who fought in France. When he returned from the war he was shell-shocked. He and I were good friends. We slept in the same room. When he came home, I welcomed him to my room, although, it was his room by right, I suppose. He said, "You and I are going to be companions here. There's something I want to tell you. If you come in, and I don't care when you come in, when you open the door, you say, 'This is John'. Don't forget to say that because if you don't I might be capable of thinking that you're a thief, or someone after me. And then, I'm very quick on the trigger." Which indeed he was. He slept with his pistol under his pillow, and I slept with my Bible under mine, so we were well protected. He and I were very good friends, but once in a while he'd have too much drink. When he did, there was more intrigue.

He took a dislike to his brother in those times of his life when he had been indulging too much. On this particular occasion, I was already in the room reading. He came in and said, "I'm going to do it tonight." "And what are you going to do tonight?" I asked. "That brother of mine," he said, "I'm going to fix him." Then he went and got his revolver. He said he wanted to test the gun underneath in the subway first and he wanted me to go with him. I said, "All right, let's go." I was quicker than he was, and when I got downstairs, his brother was there. I told him what was happening and he said it was better if we all get out, but before we could, the brother with the gun came downstairs. He forgot about going down to test his revolver when he got to the kitchen. He said he was hungry but he didn't see any of the women folk there to cook for him, and he flew into a temper. I said, "Look here, man, you and I could live if there was never a woman in the world. How many eggs would you like?" He liked eggs, I knew that. He ordered six eggs. As I fried the eggs, his brother crept through the door and gently pulled the revolver from his pocket. Away he went with the revolver. When the shell-shocked brother finished eating and went to get his revolver to test, it wasn't there. Now he was really in a rage. I got him calmed down and persuaded him to go upstairs to bed. I said, "That's the best place to be. I'm going to go myself. Come on." And he went with me, just like a child, and went to bed. There was no more trouble with the pistol after that, although his brother kept it for some time until he was in better form.

# CHAPTER 6: My Decision for the Lord

I was saved in Newry, Ireland, when I was about 21 years old. My father started some special meetings at that time. He was a gospel preacher. A Mr. McGaw and my father had rented a place in which to hold meetings. I started to attend those meetings when I was free, but there was another object in my life. I was busy working on a new invention at that time with another young man. Most of my time was taken up with that. When I'd finish work, I would begin working on this new invention. We were making a little progress on it, although it was very slow. When my boss had first said that they would like me to go to Newry for about three weeks, I had left my study books behind me. I had left my experimental apparatus behind; all the magnets, the wheels, the pulleys and everything else. I packed them up and left them to one side. I told myself that I would have a real holiday, I wouldn't think of such things. I'd come back with my head clear and better fitted out to go ahead with the real work of my life, which I thought at that time to be inventing; however, when I got to Newry, instead of being there for three weeks, I was there for three years. After getting the power station in order, they asked if I could do some other work for them; put in an extra dynamo and rewire the main switchboard, which I was very happy to do. I also repaired a pneumatic financial system in a large store. When a customer would give the clerk money, he would put it into a cartridge and send it through a tube to a central place where the money was counted. Some of the tubes were sticking but I soon put that in perfect working order. I performed many other jobs as well in Newry. Many businesses couldn't operate if they didn't have electricity and expert help was scarce. They'd come running to me when they got into trouble.

I was busy in that way and had forgotten all about the invention. Thank the Lord for that. The first Saturday that I was there, I had nothing to do, so I went out for a walk. I walked along the river's edge and while I did I began to think. I thought about my future and some verses that I had repeated and learned in Sunday school as a boy. I had heard the gospel preacher use them often: "What should it profit a man if he should gain the whole world and lose his own soul?" What would it profit me if this big invention was successful. What if I should live to be 100, and do so many great things that the papers would publish column after column on the wonderful things that I had done in my life? What would it profit, because when I would die, I would open up my eyes in Hell. That's where I would be. I knew that. I knew it as a boy in Sunday school. I heard it on my mother's knee. I heard it in the gospel meetings. I knew it to be a fact. I knew I was not ready to meet God in my sins. While the world was reading about all those wonderful things that I had done, I would be weeping in Hell. That made me think hard; however, it soon passed from my mind.

One day, while I was at my work, a gentleman came and introduced himself. He said that I didn't know him but that he had known my father well. "I preached along with him for many years," he said. "My name is Moneypenny, and I'm starting some meetings in Bessbrook. I would like you to come and attend the meetings." Bessbrook was a place two miles away from Newry. I said I'd be very happy to attend when I was free. I will be free on Sunday and Wednesday nights, I told him.

I attended those meetings and I listened. He suited my disposition very well as a preacher. He awakened me. He was a wonderful man. I had become more and more taken up with earthly things at that time. He brought the gospel out in a very clear way. First of all, he spoke about my need. He told that we were all sinners before God, that our lives would be recorded and would all be before us after death. If we died in our sins, we'd ultimately be punished because of them. I began to think more seriously on spiritual things. I used my bicycle to go to the meetings, and there was no place to keep a bicycle outside. It had to be brought in and left at the back of the hall, but this night someone had taken it right up to the front. Therefore, after the meeting ended, I couldn't get out until everybody else was out, until the front had cleared. While I was waiting, Mr. Moneypenny spoke to me and asked if I was saved yet. I said, "No." I knew I wasn't. He said, "Why not. What age are you?" I told him. "Do you not think it's time?" I said, "Yes, I do." He marked some passages in the Bible for me to read when I got home and prayed with me.

When I got home, the other boys tried to make a little fun of me for going to church. Well, that was all right with me. I went to bed and read the verses that Moneypenny had given to me, and I also began to read at Revelation, Chapter 1. I read right through until I came to Revelation, Chapter 22, almost all the book. My idea was to try and get anxious, to get serious, to get myself to think of spiritual things, but it didn't work. When I got to near the end of the book, my thoughts were back to this invention again. I had been making some improvements on it. In later years that very same concept that I had worked on was perfected by some British naval engineers, and it's working to this day. The idea was to use an electromagnet in a submarine or boat to cause a torpedo to miss. The magnet would have such an effect upon it that it would steer away from the boat or submarine. I had the invention complete in my mind's eye; all was ready. I tested it out in my mind.

I stood at the switch with another electronic apparatus that was to tell me where the missile was coming from so that I'd know the precise moment to power the magnets in such a way that the torpedo would miss its mark. Lives would be saved and the boat wouldn't be torpedoed. As I had my hand on the imaginary switch, I thought to myself, suppose it doesn't work? If it doesn't work, the whole ship is going to be blown up, and I'd be blown up with it. Even though I had been reading Revelation, I still couldn't get my thoughts to remain on spiritual things. I went to sleep crying.

The next morning I had to be up at five. When the alarm went off I jumped out of bed and got off to work to get the electricity on for everybody else in town. Then I came back for breakfast. When I came through the door, I saw the morning paper sitting on the table. I had no thoughts of what had happened the night before; not of the Gospel meeting, nor my own thoughts after reading in Revelation. I lifted up the morning paper and the first words I read were, "Johnny Hartley dies of wounds received in action." Those words hit me like a torpedo. They reached my heart and conscience. That was during World War I, about 1917. Johnny was a companion of mine. I went to Sunday school with him and, in fact, I had had tea with him three weeks before. He had been sent out to fight in France and he was just three weeks out before he was killed. Then I thought, what should I next be called? Where will my soul forever be when once my time is gone? These were the thoughts that filled my heart. I sat down with a weary heart, finished breakfast, and went back to work again.

The work that morning took me down into the subway, an underground work space. I went down with a heavy heart, wondering if I would never be saved. In fact, I then had made up my mind that I never would be saved because I never could think long enough on spiritual things. I entered the underground and walked around the passage. I fell down on my knees and sent up a prayer to God. "Oh God, have mercy on a poor guilty sinner like me. I'm afraid there's going to be no salvation for me. I can't think on these things. I can't get serious about them." Just then, I remembered a hymn that was often sung. I said the lines of that hymn: "He bore on the tree the sentence for me. He did that for me." I thought, why should I worry anymore? He did it for me. I couldn't do it for myself. He did it. And then I remembered that I could only be saved by faith, and the finished work of the Lord Jesus Christ. I realized, "I'm saved!" I can remember that moment very well. I was there in that subway underneath that big store. I couldn't stand up straight because there was no room, but I jumped for joy and my head hit the ceiling of that subway. I remember it well. I was free and I jumped for joy. And, you know, I've been jumping ever since because I'm saved and on my way to heaven. I never can forget that morning. I know the place; I see it yet:

> 'Twas in a little Irish town
> One bright September morn,
> When papers filled with awful news
> Came from the fields of France.
> Sad were the stories they did tell
> Of those poor wounded men
> Who crossed the line of that sad scene
> Into the great beyond.
> 'Twas then the awful fact did dawn –
> What should you next be called?
> Where would your soul forever be
> When once your time was gone?
> The Law came down; what did it do?
> It just condemned me through and through;
> But Jesus came blessed be His Name –
> And settled sin's tremendous claim.
> That morn I never can forget
> And, oh, the place I see it yet
> Where Jesus met me at Hell's door
> And plucked me from the burning shore.

That was my experience of salvation, right there underneath

the earth, not in a gospel hall, not in a church, not with a company of people around me, but all alone in that dark place. I took my place as a sinner and received Christ as my Savior. I was a new man in Christ Jesus. All old things were passed away, and all things had become new. Then earthly things were fading away. My old companions, fare ye well, I will not go with you to Hell. I mean with Jesus Christ to dwell for all eternity. I can remember that very well. That made the change in my life completely. After that, the poor things of this earth, no matter how great they were, hadn't the same attraction for me. I was a new man. I had other interests in life, interests that were of more value, interests that would be of real value, not only to myself but to many others, too.

The time came that I left Newry, and went on to Belfast. There were two weeks there that I had nothing to do. Now that was something for me, for I was always busy. The fact of the matter was, I was too busy. That was one of the great hindrances in my life, as I look back on it; I always kept too busy. I went during those two weeks and sat down in a park, a botanic garden. The birds were singing in the trees. It was a wonderful sight to see the green of the various leaves and the flowers. As I sat there, I began to listen to the birds sing in the trees, and I took out a paper and pen and jotted down these words.

> I sat within the Park one day,
>     Beneath the shaded wall,
>     And listened to the birdies sing
>     Up in the trees so tall.
> "There's work to do," they seemed to say,
>     "The Master doth Thee call,
>     So up and work while yet tis day
>     Ere evening shadows fall."

I remember that well. They came automatically. I had no difficulty in penning the words. Where they came from, I did not know, but I penned them in that way. Then again, as I went for a walk along the River Largon I stopped, took out the paper and pen, down went the words:

> I lingered by the river's brink
>     and heard the waters murmur low.
>     Souls are carried by the stream
>     down to Hell's fierce burning scene.

I remember jotting those words down. Then another day, as I was visiting Newcastle once more, I got out the paper and pen

again. As my eyes scanned the sea where I'd seen so many ship-
wrecks in days gone by, I began to write down:

> I stood close by the bright blue sea
>     and there the waves did shout to me,
>     "Men are drowning, can't you see them?
>     Throw the lifeline out to save them."
>
> I stood upon the mountaintop
>     And scanned the whole world o'er.
>     I saw all ruined in the fall,
>     rush on to Hell's dark door.
>
> I sat upon a soft armchair
>     and planned for future rest,
>     when in a still small voice I heard,
>     "Go ye and tell the rest."
>
> "Go ye to God's own far-off lands
>     and spread the news abroad.
>     Go ye and tell to all mankind
>     that Christ died for the lost."
>
> I got the message. I must go,
>     Else Jonah's doom befall me.
>     So keep me not, I pray thee no,
>     For God Himself hath called me.

That was God speaking to me, trying to get me to understand
that there was work to do, work that was very important indeed
in other parts of the world. And that He was sending me out
there.

# CHAPTER 7: Sunny California, and a New Work

Father's health was still a problem, and I also had a sick brother and sister. Father had a brother and sister who had lived for many years in California. They kept writing to him to go there as they thought the climate would suit him much better. So, in 1921, we all left Ireland for sunny California. It was a journey of over two weeks. It took one week on the boat to New York. There we had the joy of seeing an aunt who had lived in the U.S. for some time. Then we traveled over one week on the train to Los Angeles. Mother made our food on the train, which consisted generally of sandwiches and tea. My job was to buy the food as we passed through the towns on our way.

Sometimes, I almost missed the train, but I was always able to make it back from town. Arriving in Los Angeles, we were met by father's sister who kindly took us to her home. She gave us all a space to sleep until we found a house to rent. In two days, my brother and I found work. In a little over a week we were living in our own rented house. My other brother had to keep to bed. His back was so painful some suggested he see a chiropractic doctor, but that only made him worse. Another doctor put him in a cast where he lay for some considerable time. Finally, a nurse that father had known years ago back in Ireland passed through Los Angeles. Father invited her to our home. When she saw Hugh, she suggested that he should see her doctor. Arrangements were made, and Hugh was taken to the hospital. The doctor was able to perform a slight operation on his back and suggested that he lie in bed for two weeks; then he would come to see him. At the end of the two weeks the doctor came, examined him and pronounced him cured, but he would have to learn to walk again. He instructed my father and myself in what to do to help him. In two weeks time, right enough, there he was walking as straight and perfect as any of the rest.

My sister also found work, that is, my sister who was healthy. Our other sister remained at home and helped in the house. My sister who worked took ill and, after some considerable time, had to go to Olive View Hospital. There she was treated. She spent several years having operations in that hospital. Finally, one night, we were called to her bedside. She was not responding from one operation that she had had. The doctors thought there was little hope. They were reopening the wound to see if they could find anything. Yes, they found something they had accidentally left in after the operation. After removing that object, my sister remained in bed for some time, very sick indeed. Eventually she improved. So much that she was able to come home. She did not have to go to the hospital again, but was able to keep at home without doing any work. Then my other sister found a job. She seemed to be better in health. She was the main support of the family in many ways.

I had been thinking of many things; however, one thing that always remained with me was I felt the Lord's call to go and sound forth the wondrous story of the Lord Jesus Christ. Pretty soon, the way opened up. I had been distributing tracts around our locality near east Los Angeles. Gospel meetings were started by my father whose health, I might add, had been much improved. In fact, the climate seemed to agree with him and he was able to preach again. The tent was pitched in several places in and around Los Angeles. On one occasion, he joined up with Mr. William J. McClure and they had meetings on York Boulevard. There, I helped all I could. My work was from seven in the morning until three-thirty. I would come directly to the York Boulevard vicinity at three-thirty after work, where I distributed invitations and gospel tracts. I helped in the meetings in every way that I could. Soon I had quite a number of children in the tent to have a Sunday school while the tent was there. Later on, an assembly was formed in that parish.

I was also attracted to the Mexicans. Passing through their district after arriving in Los Angeles, I inquired who they were. They seemed to be very poor, living in old shacks partly made of wooden boxes, old tents and a little canvas. I noted where they were and eventually made my way back, having received some good gospel tracts in Spanish. Of course, Spanish was their language. I got to know the children on the streets. I had little verses made; John 3 and 16, and many more. I gave them these slips of paper with the gospel verse written on them. If they repeated that verse when I returned the following week, I gave them a little prize. At the same time, I was distributing some New Testaments which the Bible House of Los Angeles had on sale at half-price. All the young folks in the assembly got to know what I was doing. They helped in many ways by prayer, by writing out verses in English on slips of paper and also by buying some New Testaments. I kept this up and, at last, I rented a house for forty dollars a month. I also, of course, had to help at home so there was not so much money left after paying the rent of this extra house for the Mexican children. It was very interesting work, but soon it was rather rough. Some big boys had come and disturbed the meetings. The parents wouldn't allow their children to walk home alone so I had to take them home after the meeting. Finally, I rented another place in another part of the Mexican district which seemed to be a little quieter. There I had 75 to near 100 children. I went out every week and had a service for them. During the week, I would also go out to that district and distribute gospels and gospel tracts in the homes of the people. Pretty soon, they got to know me. They gained confidence in me and began to send their children to the little school which I had for them.

About that time, father and Mr. Dempsey had gospel meetings in a tent which they pitched on Central Avenue. I was at the door, of course. One night, after all the people had congregated inside and no one else was coming, I went to the street to distribute tracts and invite the people to come in. One man I had asked to come said yes. His wife had been there the night before and now it was his turn. That dear man eventually received Christ as his Savior, so did his wife and her sister. His name was Adam Trophy. As time went on Adam began to find out that I was occupied in the Mexican district. He wanted to know if he could come, too. "Of course you can," I said. In fact, it was rather difficult to get any help at all. All the young people seemed to be very busy; they seemed to have so much to do; there was no time for such a thing. Although, I must say, some of them did help. One of these dear young men was a boy by the name of Don Tyler. He came out and helped at times, but there was no one permanent to help, except the Trophys. Adam Trophy, his wife and her sister came out and took quite an interest in those dear people. We had found a better place to hold the meetings, and they practically took full charge, for which I was very thankful. At the same time, I was busy distributing gospel tracts in other parts of the Mexican district. That was about the time I began to get more and more exercised about those dear people. I had thought of going down to Mexico, where indeed there was great need. I also heard about the need in Guatemala, and that's where we eventually went.

# CHAPTER 8: A Wife and the Decision to Go

In my time working among the Mexicans I was receiving gospel tracts (*Las Buenas Nuevas* or "The Good News") from Pasadena. A young lady had come to live in Pasadena from Scotland. She had been for some little time in Canada and Cleveland. The way opened for her to come to Los Angeles, and she naturally looked up the assembly in Los Angeles. She lived beside these dear Christians who were sending me the tracts. Eventually, one of those dear sisters, Miss Ulrich, asked her if she knew a young man by the name of Ruddock who went to her assembly. She said she did. "Would you please ask him to come out and see me? I've been sending him these packages of gospel tracts for the Mexicans for some time, and I would like to hear how he is doing among those people," her neighbor asked. The message was delivered, and I was very happy indeed. I was pleased to see Miss Ulrich and her sister who was also occupied in the work, Mrs. Kinsman. This young lady was there, too. Her name was Nettie Baird.

We had much in common. I gave a description of the work I was doing and she took very much interest in the account. Finally, she, too, came out to the Mexican district. She told me that the Lord had been calling her, she thought, down to South America; however, my mind was in Mexico. So we divided it up, and went eventually to Central America.

Before we went to Guatemala, of course, we were united in marriage. The marriage took place in Pasadena. After the marriage we went on a honeymoon trip. We traveled by train up to San Francisco and Oakland. We visited the assemblies there. Then we went on to Seattle and Portland and further on up into Canada. We had a wonderful time as we visited the assemblies, telling them about the work that we had been doing. We also told them that the way seemed to be opening for us to go to Guatemala. We also went over to Vancouver Island and visited most of the assemblies there. After our trip, we returned back home to Los Angeles. Upon returning, I gave notice to my employer that I would be leaving sometime soon. Before that, they had approached me and offered a better job. There was an opening for a man to take on a greater responsibility, and I was the man they wanted to give the work to. I would need to study a little more, and they had made provision for that. They were going to send me to college where I would study and then I would be in a condition to take this work. I did not care for that, of course, but I must say that it was indeed quite a struggle within myself. I would have had a very good job indeed. I would have had a good salary, and they described what I could have done with the money. I could have had a nice home, well furnished. I'd have been well taken care of for life.

Ironically, the man they sent me to see to tell me about all this was named Mr. Worldly. When he was introduced to me as Mr. Worldly, I began to think. Worldly, where have I heard that name before? Then I remembered it was a name from *Pilgrim's Progress*, and that put me on my guard at once. Had he had another name, I might have had a more difficult time in the decision, but with a name like Worldly I couldn't mistake it. I had to make a choice between the world and God: what God wanted me to do and what the world would have me do. I told this dear man after he had spoken to me for some considerable time that it was hopeless, that I had already made up my mind what my life's work would be. I did not want to deceive the company for which I was working. If I had gone to school to learn, it would only have been for a short time. Therefore, it would be much better if they could look for someone who would be able to give all their time, energies and thoughts to the work. Very reluctantly they gave in and, of course, I was let free. Yes, I was let free, free to think seriously. I remembered a poem I had written just after I had been saved:

I heard a sweeter story
    I'm out for bigger game
Men's souls are far more precious
    Than wealth or earthly fame.

I stood upon the mountain top
    And scanned the whole world o'er.
I saw all ruined in the fall,
    Rush on to Hell's dark door.

Then I got the message, I must go,
    Else Jonah's doom befall me.
So keep me not, I pray thee no,
    For God Himself hath called me.

Those experiences came back to me in a way that gripped my soul. I couldn't get away from them; there was no escape from them. They had to be faced and, now that I had gained the victory over Mr. Worldly, I felt freer. Serious thoughts filled my mind. Both Nettie and I had labored for some time over this decision. We approached the brethren, the elders of the local assembly. We told them what was on our hearts regarding Central America and they listened very attentively. They gave us good advice; later on they would see about it. One memorable night I had been invited to go to York Boulevard in Los Angeles. That's the place I had spent so much time working in days gone by. Nettie and I went. The assembly there, along with the Jefferson Street assembly, listened very attentively to the words that I had to say. I told how I had been convinced the Lord had been calling me to fields beyond. Sometime after that, they informed me that as far as they were concerned, everything was all in order. They had looked into our lives. They could find nothing that would hinder our going, and they very kindly gave us a letter of commendation to work in Central America.

# CHAPTER 9: First Class to Guatemala and Spanish Lessons

The time drew near for our departure. We had a wonderful send off by the Christians in Jefferson Street and Avenue 54 gospel halls. We left Los Angeles in November 1926 on the Grace Line traveling by ship to Guatemala. We would sail down the Pacific Coast calling at a few ports in Mexico. A few days before sailing, I got a message to go to the office of the Grace Company Line. A gentleman wanted to see me. This gentleman was in the lumber business in Mexico. He generally traveled by train, but there was a railroad strike on in Mexico. The boat was full, and he and the agent wanted to know if my wife and I would give up our room to him and his wife as far as Mazatlan in Mexico. I would share a room with three other men and Nettie would share a room with some other ladies. Upon arriving in Mazatlan, a first class cabin would be vacant, which we would have to ourselves all the way down to Guatemala. This seemed to us to be very wonderful, so we at once made arrangements to do so.

Soon the boat pulled out from Wilmington Harbor. We had a nice time going down the Pacific. A storm came up, and we saw and heard lightning and thunder we had never experienced before. This made many of the passengers uneasy. Soon we got to Mazatlan and, as we had arranged, we transferred to the first class quarters. We were very, very comfortable there. We thanked the Lord for His kindness in making this provision for us.

As we went along we learned many helpful lessons. For instance, there was a young man on board who spoke eloquent Spanish. As we neared a port, we were met by some of the authorities. They had a little boat and, in the little boat, were some sailors. These sailors were in their bare feet; they weren't in uniform. This young man made fun of them. He was supposed to depart, but no doubt some of the authorities understood what he had said and he was not allowed into Mexico. He was forced onto the boat with the sailors and later transferred to another Grace Line ship coming back to California. At once, we caught on and learned to keep our thoughts to ourselves.

We enjoyed the trip further on, and soon we came to Champerico, a port in Guatemala, where we were getting off. There were no real docks there. The boat anchored outside and we were transferred by a crane and little basket from the boat down into one of the small boats to take us to shore. This was quite an experience. I enjoyed it very much, but other passengers did not. Soon we landed and were met by one who was to take us from there to Quetzaltenango; however, we had to pass through customs first. The man at customs did not appear to be very friendly, so much so that it was necessary for us to stay overnight, which we did not want to do. However, there was no other way out. We were allowed to take our hand baggage. The next day our luggage was passed through customs. There were no cars to take us to Quetzaltenango. The gentleman who had met us tried to make all the arrangements, but it seemed impossible. All we could do was wait. At last, he came about ten o'clock at night. He told us he had made arrangements for a special trip to Quetzaltenango. The man he hired didn't seem to care for the arrangements, so when we got out of the city a little way, the car stopped and he got out. As far as we could make out, he himself let the air out of one of the tires so that we had a flat. He told us he could go no further, he had a flat and he had no way of repairing the tire. Another car came along, and they had nothing, either. He said he would have to go back in the other car and left us sitting there. Of course, we did not know what was happening. We didn't understand enough of the language to know. I suspected this might be some kind of a holdup, so I transferred the little money that we had, which amounted to $400, out of my pocket and put it down my sock leg. I thought it would be secure there.

At last another man came along with another car and arrangements were made to take us from there up to Quetzaltenango. He was very kind. I think it was somewhere between 2:00 and 3:30 in the morning when we arrived there. Of course we were hungry and soon had something to eat. Then we were taken to our bedroom. It was rather narrow and wasn't very long, either.

It had just one door which opened to the patio in the back of the house. There were no windows to the sides, only one window in the living room that opened out to the front road. All the houses there were much the same. Nettie did not care very much for them; however, as we were now missionaries, we made up our minds we had to take things as they came. That is the best way to do it. Everything has an end. At other times in our lives we were more comfortably situated, but we were all right for the present.

Our life then was given over to the study of the language. We found a young lady there who was very capable. She helped us in a wonderful way with the language. This dear gentleman with whom we were staying turned out to be not very pleasant. We were thankful for the moment, though, knowing that all things come to an end one day. As time went on, we found that if he didn't give the order for something, it was unscriptural. Then the very thing he declared unscriptural would later on become scriptural. We came to the conclusion that it was scriptural if he agreed with it, but if he didn't agree with it, it wasn't scriptural. To me that was rather strange. His wife was not very well and seemed to be in great necessity. We very kindly helped all we could. Nettie even sold her wedding presents that she had gotten before we had left Los Angeles so that we could help them. Very soon all the money was gone, but in time the Lord very kindly came in and sent all that was necessary. Soon this dear woman had to go to the States and, afterward, her husband followed her. Then we were left all alone. We had more liberty. Life became a little more pleasant.

We went on learning the language. In nine months, I was able to give messages in Spanish; however, these messages had been translated into Spanish and then I practically read them out. The great difficulty was that when I had finished reading, the message was finished, and the meeting was over. I learned something about the culture down there through that. I had been taught, especially for the work in which I was engaged, to be punctual. So when a meeting was advertised to start at 7:00, I started at 7:00. In those days, with very few people, it was rather difficult to know if anyone would come. I got into the habit of starting the meeting at 7:00 on the minute. One night there were very few in the meeting. After I had read the message, I closed the meeting. Then, quite a number came along. They were surprised to know that the meeting was finished. Well, I said, "Don't we start at seven? I started at seven and when I finished the meeting I couldn't go on any more; my message was finished." They still came late. I once suggested that if 7 o'clock was too soon, we would have the meeting at 7:30. All right, the meeting was announced at 7:30. They still didn't come until 5 or 10 minutes after. Then I said we'd better have the meeting at 8:00; they came at 10 or 15 minutes past. I learned that it didn't matter what hour I started, there were always some people who would arrive 10 or 15 minutes late. Therefore, I began to think it wasn't the time; they have got plenty of time, but they just don't use it as we do.

Pretty soon I was able to give my messages only by using notes. This indeed made the messages more interesting and, as time went on, I didn't even need notes; however, because of circumstances outside of my control, I was not able to learn the language perfectly. I had been nearly all my life troubled with migraine headaches. I had to be very careful not to read nor study too much. In fact, that was a great drawback to the learning of the language. At times I got so frustrated that I even threw the book away. Even though I was downhearted, I was able to go right on and do what I could. So, in one way, I never did learn the language, I just grew into it. As long as I could make myself understood, that was all that was necessary. Thank the Lord for those who were able to study hour after hour and never have a pain in their head. Nettie was like that. She was able to continue with the studies hour after hour. She did not know what a headache was. Thank the Lord for that. That was wonderful because I would not like anyone to have to suffer the way I and others have done with migraine headaches. The fact of the matter is we cannot explain the pain to others. They cannot have an idea of what it means to have a gnawing headache, minute after minute, hour after hour and day after day. It knocks you out. It takes away your normal mode of thinking. You cannot even collect your thoughts at times. At times, in fact, it leaves you useless. That indeed is annoying. To think that you are no good; to think that you are holding others back; that is some pain in itself. But those who have migraine headaches, they have to put up with them. I think the Lord makes it up to them in some other way.

Thank the Lord for Nettie. She was able to pick up the Spanish perfectly. In fact, she became quite a teacher of Spanish. She has been a wonderful help to me in that line. I do not know how I would have gotten along without her language skills. She helped me so much. If there was a difficulty in the language, she would overcome it. She could explain it to me as others did not seem to have the capacity to do so. Of course, she knew my weakness. She had the patience to explain and re-explain in such a way that soon I was able, at least in some little measure, to express myself and get the message over. Soon I was able to go out and have gospel meetings in various places.

# CHAPTER 10: A Downpour of Ashes

## Notes on a Guatemalan Volcano Eruption

**6:30 p.m.** – I arrived from where I had left Mrs. Ruddock (Nettie) and the baby. The train was late. I felt tired and had a headache.

**8 p.m.** – Went to bed.

**1 p.m.** – Thought I felt soot in my mouth. Something must be on fire I said to myself, but as my headache was a little better I did not want to get up to see what was wrong in case it would start aching again, so went off to sleep with the sooty taste in my mouth.

**11:30 p.m.** – I heard someone outside my window shouting, *"Don* Juan, *Don* Juan." "What is wrong?" I said. "Shut your windows and doors," said this Christian who had come to warn me. "Santa Maria volcano is in eruption and is throwing out balls of fire and ashes. Pretty soon the ashes will be here; it is well to get all ready so as to be able to run at once if the lava should come this way." She then went on her way to warn others.

Ashes were then falling but I thought it was just like other times; however, I shut the windows and doors, and climbed to the roof of the house, to have a look at the volcano. Right enough, there it was throwing out fire and making noises like thunder. Just then the ashes began to fall thicker and heavier and I had scarcely reached the ground when a regular downpour of ashes fell fast and loud, rattling off the zinc roof like hail. I ran into my bedroom and shut the door. I opened the window to look out but had to shut it real quick. The excitement started my headache again but I thought if I should have to run, I would rather leave the headache behind me, so after taking care of things we value, I lay down again and went off to sleep.

**Sunday 3:30 a.m.** – I woke and looked out to see a white world

43

of ashes. The ashes were no longer falling but the streets were full of excited people. Rain then fell for half an hour and then ashes began to fall again for another two hours.

**6:30 a.m.** – I got up and went around to the home of one of the Christians, to see and hear the results. Two refugees had already arrived from one of the farms that suffered most, and which lies at the foot of the volcano. They left the farm about 9 p.m. the night before after seeing it ruined. Big stones and balls of fire were falling, they said, so they fled for their lives.

**7:30 a.m.** – Others arrived and told us that when they left hot water was beginning to fall. In a few moments more refugees arrived and said that an old man and woman, two children and another woman had been scalded to death.

**8 a.m.** – The ashes had stopped falling but everywhere one looked ashes were to be seen and the food tasted of ashes. A rescue party started off to the village of Palmar which lies on the skirt of the volcano and to the side of the volcano that was in action. The trucks, however, under the best of conditions, can only go a certain distance as there is no auto road. Black smoke and steam then began to shoot into the air from the crater, hundreds of feet high.

**3 p.m.** – The first of the refugee party arrived with a truckload of refugees. The driver brought terrible stories of whole families being wiped out of existence. Some were killed by the stones, others burned by the hot mud and water, etc. The load he brought was a sight. The women's hair was full of fine ashes which the rain had turned into a kind of cement. They were tired out as they had been fleeing in the dark over terrible roads that were really not roads at all. Houses were destroyed and buried. The coffee and other crops ruined, and sad were the stories told of old folks who could not run. Others did not want to leave the awful scene; no doubt because of not being able to find their loved ones, and losing others. Very soon other trucks arrived with the wounded, most of them burned.

**Monday** – Today we learned more of what happened after the heavy shower of ashes Saturday night. The volcano began to throw out fire and the hot lava began to flow carrying all before it, burying houses, animals and crops and precious souls as well. Here in San Felipe there was great excitement everywhere as no one knew just what the results of the eruption would be and the volcano still seemed to be busy. In the evening, more refugees arrived at the door of our house looking for a place to sleep. I showed them into the hall. One man had a woman on his back with both her feet burned. Another had a man on his back with both feet and hands badly burned. After making them comfortable, I had joy in telling them the old, old story. In the morning they went to the hospital while their friends stayed here. My wife not being in San Felipe, another Christian volunteered to cook for the refugees we had under our care. In this way, we cared for 28 persons. Another Christian had under her care 15 persons. We had special gospel meetings with good attendance and distributed clothing to the children. This clothing had been sent some time ago by the missionary classes. The man who lived next door to us owned a farm very near to the volcano and he only escaped with his life, while the lava burned up his car and driver before his eyes.

As soon as possible I visited the lava-swept district with gospels and tracts. What a terrible sight met the eye. What was once a fruitful mountainside was now a desert. Ashes, sand, lava, stones, etc., everywhere. Not a blade of anything green could be seen. The rescue party was still at work burying human bodies and also animals to keep a plague from starting. Those who had escaped were looking for their loved ones among the ruins, digging their bodies out from the lava under their house which had fallen on top of them. Others had been overtaken by the hot lava while fleeing for their lives. One man apparently had tried to climb a tree but was overtaken by the lava, and was found with his arms around the tree. I was told that one Christian family was found, all on their knees as though they had been praying. No doubt many were brought to their knees by the terrible catastrophe.

I distributed gospels to the rescue party and to those who were looking for their friends, talking to them as I went, about the salvation of their soul. Their hearts seemed to be much softer and they showed more interest in the gospel than they had done before when I visited them. May the Lord have mercy on those who escaped and save their souls. This district has been much against the gospel. When the calamity happened the people were just finishing up a celebration of what we might call a feast for the dead. This is supposed to be a day of mourning for the dead but they make it more of a feast than anything else.

John Ruddock
San Felipe, Guatemala
Central America
2nd November 1929

There was a village down below that volcano. The lava, the water, and the mud came down with such a rush that it buried that little village completely. It came within 10 minutes of our village; however, in the morning, the dust from the volcano was one inch thick everywhere. The volcano dust got right inside the house. The house was covered completely – furniture and everything else.

In a few days, it was possible to make our way up to the volcano. We went up and stood in the very place where the village had been. Those dear people had not a chance. They were buried alive. It happened on All Saints Day. Those dear people were celebrating. It was a religious feast, but it mixed pagan dancing and drinking and all kinds of evil. The volcano erupted and they knew nothing about it. Some of them ran, some escaped, but very, very few indeed. I think 300 lost their lives on that night.

## CHAPTER 11: A Dog Bite and a Borrowed Sweater

One day, in a Guatemalan village, while I was distributing gospel tracts and inviting people to come to a gospel meeting, I was attracted by a dog in front of me. He stood barking with his teeth bared. Of course, I thought I had better be very careful with that dog. But suddenly there was another dog behind me, and before I knew, it had me by the leg. Well, that was very painful indeed. I went back to the place where I was staying, but there was no help in that village, no doctors, no drugstores, no one with any experience. All I could find was salt, salt and dirty rags. I applied those to my leg, but it was not improving. I thought that I'd better get back home to Quetzaltenango.

In those days, traveling was done by truck. Trucks would carry goods to the various towns and, if there was room, the truck driver would, for a certain amount of money, give you a ride. I was told where I could get on a mail truck to Quetzaltenango. I arrived in the place and waited for some considerable time. The mail truck came along, but it was unable to take me as it was already well filled. Now, down there, well-filled means that people are packed in so tightly that it would be rather difficult if not impossible to squeeze another person in. When can I get another ride? I asked. Perhaps tomorrow, they said. There was nothing for me to do but start out and walk. It was a 20-mile walk with a bad leg and, I might say, it took me some considerable time. With much difficulty and pain, I eventually arrived home. There, Nettie was ready for the occasion. In a few weeks she had my leg all right again. Another time I was distributing tracts in another place, and five dogs surrounded

47

me. They were coming at me little by little and making all kinds of noises with their teeth bared. The owner of those dogs stood and laughed. At last, when he saw that there was a great necessity, he came in and controlled the dogs.

Another time in Guatemala, I distributed tracts in a little village I was unfamiliar with. After finishing, I walked on to see if there was some other village past it. I kept walking for some considerable time, about an hour I expect. As it turned out I had made a circle and come back right again to that same village. Many things come into one's life to teach us lessons to apply to the future.

Once I was invited to a wedding down the Guatemalan coast. Down on the coast, it's very hot, so hot I found it impossible to use a coat. I made just my shirt and pants do. I never even used any underwear. It was much too hot for me and the heat would bring on headaches. On this occasion, when I went to the wedding, I was not allowed to go in because I did not have a coat on. Nettie came to the rescue. She gave me her sweater, I put it on and then I could go in and attend the wedding ceremony. The ceremony was conducted by the mayor of the town. The mayor of the town I noticed was sitting in his bare feet. He had neither socks nor shoes on. I noticed he had four pens sticking out of his pocket, but his secretary performed the ceremony. After speaking for some time, he gave the license to the mayor to sign. This dear man, I noticed, signed an "X." He couldn't write, so the secretary had to do the writing, too. There was a lot to learn in Guatemala. It was rather funny though to see me sitting there with my wife's sweater on. However, it fit the occasion and saved the situation.

On another occasion there, we went to a place where prisoners were kept. These prisoners were made to work. It was a very hot place infested with many mosquitos. It was rather difficult to get out of their way. In fact, one needed to sleep covered with a mosquito net. Poor Nettie suffered on that trip. She had to get under the mosquito net with a big fat woman. The smell inside there wasn't very pleasant, but it was all in a day's work. There are many unpleasant things that come into one's life but, as I said before, everything comes to an end. In about one year's time, the gentleman of the house returned to Quetzaltenango, and we thought it would be a good time to move on to a new place.

We moved to San Felipe, Guatemala, 30 miles down on the

coast. It was rather warm there, but there were good opportunities to visit the many villages around and take the gospel to those people. We learned many more lessons as we were occupied in the work. Before long in Guatemala though, we decided our call was to be pioneering missionaries, and the Lord was opening the way further south to Honduras and the Mosquito Coast.

# CHAPTER 12: Don Alfredo, Missionary General

In his youth, Alfred Hockings was interested in the mission field, and he tried to fit himself out for that occupation. He had gone to a medical school and had taken a medical course that was suitable for missionaries. He had also fitted himself out in other ways, and was waiting for the Lord to open up a path for him to go to some foreign field. At that time, the American Bible Society needed someone, but could not find anyone in the United States, so they advertised for someone in England. Don Alfredo saw this notice. He applied and very soon was on his way down to Central America. The American Bible Society, at that time, had its headquarters in Panama.

His proper name in Spanish was Alfredo Hockings, but down in those countries you're always called by your first name. Then they add *Don* to it, which really means mister. *Don* Alfredo was his name ever after. He spent lots of time traveling through Central America: Guatemala, El Salvador, Honduras, Nicaragua, Costa Rica, and Colombia, as well as parts of Venezuela.

He had a couple of mules and a helper. One mule was for himself and the other for the Bibles. He would set out with his mule well laden with Bibles. He had spent many travels on mule back through these lands. In fact, there was no other way to travel up the steep mountainsides and down the valleys. Sometimes as he rode, he was in great danger. Sometimes he was robbed of everything. Other times he was down with malaria. He had even been stoned by persecutors.

Once, while living in Honduras, he was mistaken for a general

– a rebel general. The soldiers took him to their headquarters and imprisoned him there until their general could see him. At last, their general arrived. It turned out Don Alfredo and this general were well acquainted, so the general was surprised to see him there. The general asked him, "What are you doing here?" Don Alfredo said, "I don't know. These men of yours brought me in and they said that I was General Tosta." General Tosta was one of the rebel generals. Don Alfredo had a complexion much the same as Tosta's. Although Don Alfredo was an Englishman, and spoke Spanish, rather brokenly at that time, the soldiers had for some reason thought sure they had captured a rebel general. Don Alfredo and the general had quite a time together, the two of them, laughing over what had happened, and then the general asked him where he wanted to go. Don Alfredo said, "I want to go back home to San Pedro Sula." That's where he lived in Honduras. So the general called some soldiers and told them to prepare for the trip to San Pedro Sula to see that Don Alfredo got to his home safely, which he did.

Afterward, he returned to England for a time. First of all, though, he went to Canada to have the malaria frozen out of his body. He got married in England, and brought his young wife back with him to Honduras to the capital, Tegucigalpa. He had resigned from the American Bible Society and was going to settle down as a missionary. However, he was looking to the Lord to guide him to the proper place. There was another missionary, with a wife, living in San Pedro Sula, but this missionary could not stand the climate any longer. The doctor told him he must get out, so he made arrangements to leave, as other missionaries had before him. That part of Honduras was very, very unhealthy. No one seemed to be able to stay for any length of time. Some had to be carried out on stretchers. One dear young woman lost her life because of the malaria. In addition to malaria, there were dysentery and other tropical diseases to contend with.

When Mr. Hockings heard about this missionary's plight, he thought he would try San Pedro Sula, so arrangements were made for Don Alfredo and his wife, *Doña* Evelena, to go to San Pedro Sula. It was up one mountain, down a valley along a path beside another mountain and through another valley. In their trip, they almost lost their first-born child. The child fell from the second story of a house they were staying in. Fortunately, she was not injured.

When they arrived in San Pedro Sula, Don Alfredo took over.

At that time, there was very little work being done. There were just three or four Christians, that was all. The pioneering work had yet to be done, but Don Alfredo was doing his best. He was, of course, a colporteur and had little experience building assemblies. As he had some medical experience, he was exercised about sick people. He was able to help the sick in many ways. He made a few trips along the coast and was seeing just a little work done, but not very much. In these early days, he made a trip to Guatemala and, of course, he came to visit us. We had a very happy time with him. He got us very much interested in Honduras. He told us about the great need in Honduras – right from the border of Guatemala through Honduras to the border of Nicaragua. There were no missionaries there of any kind. It was virgin ground. There was a great need there, and that was what we were looking for. In fact, we had made up our minds that we were not going to stay long in that part of Guatemala. We had thought of going to the great Peten district. Peten was a big district in Guatemala that had not been opened up to the gospel, and that was the kind of a place I had longed for.

Don Alfredo's time went very quickly, and soon he returned to Honduras. We promised that we would visit him later on.

# CHAPTER 13: A Short Sabbatical and a Harsh New Life

I was taking trips away from home, preaching the gospel, and sometimes was away for days at a time. Once, when I returned, I found Nettie very ill and very weak. In San Felipe, there was no doctor and no pharmacy. We were pretty well left on our own. When Nettie took ill, one of the Christian sisters took it upon herself to try and help. However, she must have given her too much castor oil. Castor oil was what she needed, so she was told, but the dose was too much for her. Nettie was pregnant with our first daughter, Margaret Jean, so we moved to Guatemala City, where there was a hospital, for the birth. That was indeed the Lord's leading, although, at the time, we were much criticized for doing so. Nettie went into labor after witnessing a plane crash. The plane gave Nettie quite a fright, as it came down just two blocks from where she was standing.

We went to the American hospital there, which was run by the Presbyterian church. A very good Christian doctor examined Nettie, and felt she was all right, but when the time came, we found out that it was a very, very serious birth. In fact, the doctor approached me and told me there was little or no hope of saving the child. He said it would either be the life of the child or my wife, and I had to make the decision. Fortunately, there was an expert doctor there at the time from the United States. It was the Lord's doing, there was no doubt about that. This young man had studied and was an expert in obstetrics. He happened to be visiting Guatemala City, and that very day he should have been on the plane going back to the United States, but the night before he was taken ill with dysentery. It was impossible for him to take the trip. He knew exactly what to do and our first-born, Margaret Jean, was born normally. We thank the Lord for that. It took my wife some considerable time to recover.

The migraine headaches that had always troubled me were acting up. I remember one day as I was out distributing tracts in a little village not very far from where we lived in San Felipe, the pain was so much that I laid down on the pathway. As I lay there, I heard a rumbling noise. I looked up and saw a big stone coming down the cliff, coming right where I was. I had time to jump and nothing more. How I did it I can't tell, but I jumped back three feet all at once on my back. Just as I jumped, the big stone came down where I had been lying. That experience impressed me to take the doctor's advice and go far away for a time so I could get my health restored, and try and get relief from my headaches. This we did.

We made arrangements and set sail for Scotland. It was a memorable journey. It took us four weeks to go by boat, but it was very restful indeed. The weather was something wonderful all the way. We called at a port in Costa Rica and had the privilege of seeing the Panama Canal. We finally got to visit the people of the American Bible Society that supplied our Bibles during our time in Guatemala. We went on to Venezuela, and then to Trinidad.

In Trinidad, we heard our name called out from another boat. Some other missionaries had heard we were visiting, so we went with them for the night, and spent the next day looking around the island, hearing of the wonderful things that the Lord was doing in that place. The other poor passengers had to stay on the boat. It was taking on coal, and the coal dust wasn't very pleasant.

We eventually arrived in Plymouth, England. I had heard that one of the Plymouth Brethren there was very active in looking after visiting missionaries. I was told that I'd find him on top of a big building. I went there and, right enough, he was at the top, very busy. The only way to see him was to go up a ladder, so I headed up the 60 foot ladder. I was used to heights, so that didn't trouble me very much, but, I must confess, that it was a strange feeling when I got three-quarters of the way up. At long last, I met one of the famous Plymouth Brethren. We had a nice chat together, and then it was time for me to go.

Getting off the boat, we had to wait a little time for the train to Scotland. We were advised that we could have a lunch on the train. We put in the order and they were to give us a basket lunch at a certain place. The food was all right, but the money wasn't all right. The only currency we had was a 10 shilling gold piece, and I offered that for our food, but the boy wouldn't take it. He looked at it. He didn't seem to know what it was. Well, I said, "This is strange. This is a 10 shilling English piece. A gold piece." The poor boy hadn't seen such a thing before, but that's all the money we had. At last he took it, and went off. That left us without anything. However, when we got to Glasgow on the train, there were friends there who kindly took us to their home. Nettie was delighted. Her mother, father and sisters were there. (She did not have any brothers.)

Her mother said she wouldn't have known her had she not known that she was coming. Those years in Guatemala had taken effect. We were both very weary and run down in health. There was more bone than flesh, so no wonder she didn't know her own daughter. A short time in Scotland, however, revived us both. The headaches, although they still troubled me, didn't trouble me so much, and Nettie began to be rather famous around those parts.

During the stay in Guatemala, the Lord was able to help her in many ways. She began to be well-known as one able to take away tapeworms. Tapeworms, at that time in Guatemala, troubled many, many people, and it was a rare thing to get them cured completely. However, Nettie began to study the situation and her father was able to send her some special medicine from Scotland. This medicine had the effect of taking the tapeworm right away; head, tail and all. Some of these worms were very many yards in length. In fact, it's hard to believe that there was such a thing in a human body. So, at home in Scotland, as we traveled around, she was asked to tell of the experience. She became a rather popular speaker indeed.

Meanwhile, I made arrangements to go over to Ireland. I was invited to speak at a conference. I spoke along with Ernie Wilson, my old companion. He had been out to Central Africa and had had quite an experience there. The Lord blessed his words as they went forth and many souls were saved. He had quite a story to tell, and we had a good time together.

As I went around telling the dear people what there was yet to be done in Central America, quite an interest was stirred up. Pretty soon Nettie joined me in Ireland and we had a wonderful time together. At every house we visited we had to have a cup of tea and an egg and some other nice dainties to eat, until Nettie couldn't stand it any longer. At night when we thought everything was over, we were invited to go for that last evening and see some more Christian friends. We had a very happy time there indeed. We left our little girl, Margaret, about 11 months of age, with her grandmother in Scotland, while we were in Ireland.

From Scotland we all went to New York, once more by boat. We spent a little time there with my aunt and a cousin who was also living there at that time. This cousin was a wonderful help, as she knew New York perfectly and was able to take me on the subway to visit many of the assemblies. I had the great joy of telling them how the Lord had called me to the work in Guatemala, but we were now thinking of going back to Honduras, not Guatemala. After spending some time in New York, we took the train and visited several places as we came on the way to California once more. We visited many of the assemblies on the way and made many good friends. When the train got to Pomona, California, a strange sight caught our eyes. There, in big letters, I read, "John and Nettie Return From Guatemala." It was some of the dear Christians who came out to meet us from Los Angeles, and they were playing this trick on us, making us believe that the authorities were giving us a welcome home to Los Angeles.

There was a happy welcome for us in Los Angeles. All the dear Christians couldn't do enough for us. Some dear sisters in the missionary class had made up special poems for us. We spent some time there visiting the little assemblies that we had known before we went out to Guatemala. My family was all intact, and we had a wonderful time with them. My brother, who had such a time with his back, seemed to be still well cured, and was working and helping, and my other sister, who had been ill in Ireland, seemed to be all right and was working, too. My father even, who was so weak in Ireland, now seemed to have revived his youth. He, too, was busy preaching the gospel in many places around Los Angeles, especially in tents in the tent revival season. But we had to say goodbye at last to those at home in Los Angeles.

This time we were going to Honduras direct from Los Angeles. We had to go to New Orleans to get a boat. On the way, we visited more assemblies. We passed through Houston. We made many good friends there who were friends for years after. In

New Orleans, in those days, there were not many Christians, but that's where we got the United Fruit Company boat bound for Honduras. We had a very nice trip down. We arrived at Puerto Cortes, Honduras. Don Alfredo was there to meet us.

Of course, we had to pass through customs, but we got there rather late in the evening so it wasn't possible for us to get through customs that night. As it turned out, one of the head men of the customs was a Christian. He allowed us to get off the boat that night and take our hand baggage with us. Don Alfredo had made arrangements for us to stay in a Christian's home in that Caribbean port. We went to that home and what do you know, the whole family of six or seven children had the whooping cough. They coughed and they coughed and they coughed. Our little girl never did have the whooping cough, so she was in danger of being infected. However, the Lord kept her well.

We were to be up very early the next morning, about five o'clock. We found the baggage was already off, but we had to get it over to the railroad station because there was a train from that port up to San Pedro Sula. There was no road at that time, only the railroad. Now first we had to buy tickets to take us up to San Pedro Sula. Don Alfredo did his best to get the tickets. We had already taken my wife and little girl and got them seated in the train. We then went back to wait for the ticket office to open to buy the tickets. When the office did open, there was an argument going on. The man who was supposed to be selling the tickets didn't seem to be much interested in selling tickets. He was more interested in arguing with this old man about something. Don Alfredo tried to attract his attention.

Finally, Don Alfredo said to me, "Look here, I'm afraid we're not going to get away today. You'd better go and get your wife off the train." So I ran back and got Nettie and Margaret off the train. No sooner had we got them off the train then the train left for San Pedro Sula. When we came back to Don Alfredo, the ticket man said, "Well, that's all right. There's another train tomorrow." Well, that was all right for him, but for us, what were we to do in the meantime? That was another lesson in "mañana" (the Spanish word for tomorrow). We would hear much more of it. Don Alfredo then thought it would be best to go and find some other place to sleep that night. It was rather hot down there in the port. We had to walk. We did a lot of walking. After about three-quarters of an hour's walk, carrying our hand baggage, we got to another Christian's home. There they very kindly took us in and gave us a place to sleep. Of course, they made some food for us, and we were all right then. We couldn't buy the tickets until the next morning.

Bright and early we were down at the station and, right enough, this time the argument was over, whatever it was about. The man who sold the tickets didn't have anything else to do, so he sold us our tickets. Then we were able to get the baggage onto the train. In Pedro Sula, we had to make arrangements to get our baggage off the train. There were no taxis there. There were no cars at all there at that time. We had to look for a horse or a mule and a wagon. Eventually, we made it up to Don Alfredo's home. There wasn't very much room in it. However, we were given a room to ourselves. Mrs. Hockings very kindly made us some food. Fortunately, the Lord had supplied us with some money before leaving the States. It was very plain to see that they were in very poor circumstances. We found that their beds weren't really beds. They were an imitation of a bed. We found out that underneath their beds, they had put their trunks. On top of the trunk they had an old, old mattress. That's what they were sleeping on. We soon made arrangements so that they could have a real mattress.

We were there for some little time. We were able to help a little in the work. Don Alfredo had been at home for some time, looking after a sick boy, but the sick boy had passed away. Now he wanted to go out and visit some of his old friends, so I volunteered to stay at home and look after the meetings there, which indeed were very, very small at that time. In the meantime, my wife and I had been looking around and found a better place to live. We rented it and moved in.

# CHAPTER 14: A Missionary Welcome

This song was written for John and Nettie Ruddock to be sung as a welcome on the occasion of their first return to Los Angeles since their wedding and departure for the mission field in 1926. It was now 1931. They had left Guatemala for a sabbatical in Britain and then Los Angeles, and subsequently returned to search out the Mosquito Jungle area of Honduras and start a new work there.

### A Missionary Welcome

*You were constrained thro' love of Christ*
*His mercies to proclaim,*
*Your cherished hopes you sacrificed*
*To spread abroad His fame.*

*'Twas with rejoicing mixed with tears,*
*We saw you sail away,*
*But praise our God, He answered prayers,*
*And kept you all the way.*

*Now welcome home, ye harvest lab'rers,*
*Joyful hearts with praises ring;*
*Welcome home from lands of darkness,*
*Welcome home to you we sing.*

*You labored on thro' weary years*
*Dispelling sin's dark night,*
*You scattered sunshine, banished fears,*
*And spread the Gospel light.*

59

'Twas with rejoicing that we learned
God blessed your toils of love;
And souls to Christ from idols turned,
To serve the Lord above.

Now welcome home, ye harvest lab'rers,
Joyful hearts with praises ring;
Welcome home from lands of darkness,
Welcome home to you we sing.

How often as you labored there,
Our tho'ts to you would turn,
How oft we followed you with prayer,
And longed for your return.

O, what rejoicing then we knew
When you were homeward bound,
Thrice welcome home we sing to you,
O let the word resound.

Now welcome home, ye harvest lab'rers,
Joyful hearts with praises ring;
Welcome home from lands of darkness,
Welcome home to you we sing.

# CHAPTER 15: *In Search of the Mosquito District*

As time went on, I had become more desirous of visiting the Mosquito District, otherwise known as the Mosquito Coast. (A dense jungle area that marks the border between Honduras and Nicaragua and that offered sanctuary to Contra guerrillas battling the Sandinistas in recent years; it was largely unexplored at that time.) I had heard of it, but knew little about it. No one, in fact, seemed to know very much about it. I had been interested in, as I already said, the Peten district in Guatemala, and the Mosquito District in Honduras, because these two districts were wastelands. In fact, part of Honduras down there was unmapped and hadn't been properly inhabited. I was much interested in the Mosquito Indians who lived in that area. We tried to find out how to get there. That was one place that Don Alfredo had not been, even the authorities did not know much about it. We were told we would have to go to Tegucigalpa (the capital of Honduras), and make our way from there to the Mosquito District. Don Alfredo volunteered to go along with me.

At that time the train that I've already spoken about from Puerto Cortes to San Pedro Sula went on still further to a place by the name of Potrerillos, which was not very far. In fact, the whole line was about 60 miles or so from Puerto Cortes. When we got to Potrerillos, we had to take a truck from there. The truck was a *baronesa*. It carried the mail going up to Tegucigalpa. There was no railroad up into Tegucigalpa at that time. However, that truck took us part of the way. When we came to Lake

Yojoa, there was no road around the lake so we were put on a boat; a boat large enough to carry this baronesa. It took us about two hours or so to cross that lake. It was quite a big lake, very beautiful, indeed. I enjoyed the trip because it was very peaceful. At the other end, the baronesa was taken off the boat, then we made our way by road from there. You wouldn't call it a road, perhaps, but it was passable. In fact, it was rather dangerous.

Don Alfredo was a man who had faced many dangers, but one thing he did not like to do was sit on the outside of a baronesa. He liked to get into the middle of the truck so he couldn't see, for sometimes, actually, one thought they were going over the cliff, right down hundreds of feet below. In fact, many of those baronesas, which were used to take provisions up to the capital of the country, Tegucigalpa, went right over the cliff. We made our way up and it was rough going but exciting and beautiful. We had left the low-lying hot, humid coast and were now traveling up in the mountains. The road is cut out of the mountainside and, in places, is very narrow – so narrow that two cars could not pass each other. At times like this, one must be very careful, indeed. The road is also very rocky, with lots of stones. It is impossible to go at any speed. On and on we went up this road, around bends, some of them switchbacks. There you must go as far as possible, then back up, and then try and get around the next turn.

We passed through some very small villages. They were very thinly populated up in the mountains; not as many people as down on the coast where there was lots of work to be found on the banana plantations. Here, the people lived on a little piece of ground that they had cut out for themselves. They grew corn, just enough to supply their own needs. They also grew black beans, and, of course, there was a little coffee in some of these places, too. We kept on until we passed through Taulavey. Taulavey is a little larger than most villages. There's a cave there. It is not completely explored, even as yet. However, they're currently making efforts to get it into condition so that tourists will have the pleasure of seeing it. The higher we climbed the cooler it got. Up and up we went and very soon we saw Siguatepeque appear.

Siguatepeque is a little city. It is situated halfway between San Pedro Sula and Tegucigalpa. There's a big district around it, where small farmers earn their living by growing corn and black beans. Higher up, they even grow potatoes, but they're very small. They're not very good, either. Siguatepeque was our journey's end for the day. We got there about five o'clock in the afternoon. We went to the motel. All the passengers slept there at night, both coming and going from Tegucigalpa and San Pedro Sula. It was the halfway point. It was an old-fashioned motel with old-fashioned rooms. Although you wouldn't call it very much at all, it was to me at least a very welcome sight. The beds were not, of course, as we are now used to, but we were able to have a good night's rest. The food, of course, was a little different from what we got on the coast: It was rice and beans, a little beef and some soup, as well as tortillas. And, sometimes, when some foreigner came in, they made every effort to bake a little loaf of bread. They had white butter, which is very good. We spent one day in that place, looking around. I was very anxious to see what was there. Brother Hockings, of course, knew the place well, as he had passed through there many times in his work as a colporteur. There was what was known as a Central American mission there. They had established themselves there sometime before. Right from San Pedro Sula on the coast to the border of Nicaragua, there were no missions going on whatsoever. We were, from the beginning, on our own on the coast, but up here it was a little different. We soon got to know that they claimed this part of the country and they discouraged any other missionaries from working there. That was made very plain to us, although those we met were very kind and helpful in many other ways. There were very few real believers, but it was a start. The next morning, early, about four o'clock, we started off on our journey again.

This time we left for Tegucigalpa. The road stayed bad. We went up one mountain and down another. One mountain was rather high. There were many turns in it. As you went around that mountain to get up to its top and over to the other side, one met with other trucks on their way to San Pedro Sula. Going up one of these hills, my hat blew off. They went back and got my hat and apologized for running over it and knocking it a little out of shape, but that wasn't the worst of it. As we went on a little further, we discovered that they were losing mail, too. This truck also carried letters and small packages from one post office to another. Something had happened with the back door of the baronesa, and mail started falling out, so we had to stop, go back and try to pick up the lost mail. Some of it was over and down the precipice. It was lots of fun gathering it together. Eventually, all was in order again. At some of these hills, the driver stopped and took on water. The radiator would boil. Back in those years it was necessary to stop every once in awhile to fill up with water, and sometimes it was necessary to stop for quite awhile until the engine cooled down.

We soon were up in the pine trees. We could see nothing but pine trees there, all over. Whereas, on the coast, it would be bananas, bananas, and more bananas, wherever you went, but here it was pine trees. Then, nearer and nearer we came, until at last we were to the top. As we looked down on the valley below, we could see Comayagua. Yes, there it was, another fair-sized place. This was the capital of the country at one time. It's quite a place for Roman Catholic churches. Some of these churches are very costly. Some of them have gold roofs that glitter in the sun. There are many antiques in these places, too, but we were not so much interested in that. We were not altogether back to sea level in this valley, but almost. It was rather hot again, but not nearly as hot as down on the coast. We were able to visit another mission there. The missionaries made it clear and plain that they were in control of that place. They had been doing a little work, but it was very, very little indeed, considering the number of people who were there. The people farmed corn and beans there, as in Siguatepeque.

This was the last stage of the trip up to Tegucigalpa. Up here, of course, the houses are different than down on the coast. They're more substantial in many ways. They're built of adobe. It's colder up here, and they need better protection, but there are very few windows. In fact, there may be only one very small window in a little house. The doors are all barred from the inside to try to make it safe. As we went along, Mr. Hockings entertained me by telling me of what had happened to him in many of these places as he had traveled that way by mule selling Bibles. He told me how thieves had taken everything from him, or how they stole his mule just as we passed the crime scenes. That dear man had been robbed many times as he went about in years gone by selling the Bibles. Of course, at this time, it was a little better. There was a road now. At that time there was no road, only a mule path. The nearer we got to Tegucigalpa the better the road was. On we went. At last we came to a big hill and, as we looked down from that hill, there we could see Tegucigalpa.

Tegucigalpa is really two cities in one. There is Tegucigalpa and Comayaguala. These are, you might say, big villages, but they're separated by the river Comayagua. As we got nearer we could see that we were traveling in the dry season because everything was so dusty. Dust was everywhere. Whereas, in the wet season, there would be mud, mud everywhere. Sometimes, as we went along, we had to eat our own dust coming from the baronesa as we turned sharp and went back up or down. As we passed through Comayaguala, first of all, we saw the river. That river was the laundromat for all of that part of the country, and it was some sight to see, early in the morning, women all busy washing their clothes and stretching them out on the dry stones of the river, all colors, all shapes, all kinds of wearing material. In their houses there was no water. There was a central water tub outside in one of the squares. They'd make their way there with water containers, fill them up and carry them back to the house. The women folk did most of that kind of work. They carried everything on their heads. It was wonderful to see each one coming, one after the other, with a pail or basin with water set on their head. Their homes had earthen floors. There was no luxury in these homes. Only, of course, in a few houses of those who were richer. There were actually quite a lot of rich people there. There are more now, however, than there were back in 1930. The government men and the ambassadors from other countries were able to erect more permanent and more luxurious homes, but our work was with the poor people so we made our way to where they were. And they were very hospitable indeed.

As we went and visited around we found three or four existing missions. They claimed all that part of the country. It seemed that they had divided the country among themselves. That is the highlands, and the climate is good up there. They all seemed to pick out those parts because it was cool. They left the hot coast to us. We were given to understand that that was our territory. As Don Alfredo would often say, we had our mission to go into all the world. We had our hands full down on the coast. There was a big open door there and plenty to do so we didn't take so very much interest in the upper, higher ground at that time.

We spent some limited time in Tegucigalpa. We visited the central park. Every city or town has a central park in Honduras. Tegucigalpa had several. People went to the park to relax in the afternoons and evenings. It was a custom there for young people to congregate in these parks. All the houses had iron bars to keep thieves out and to be a protection in the time of revolution. Any house that was of any value had its doors well barricaded. The windows were also barricaded with these iron bars. The houses were narrow in the front. There was a big door called the *san wan*. That was the principal door into these houses. It didn't lead you right into the house though, it led you into a patio in the center of the house. Any house would have beautiful flowers and plants in that patio. Around the patio were the bedrooms, the living room and, way at the far end, the kitchen quarters. As you walked along you would see, perhaps, a nice young lady inside behind the bars, and a young man outside on the street. He was flirting with this young lady there; he on the street and she inside. That was the way things were done at that time. In the evenings or at night, all those young people would come out to the park. The young ladies would be escorted. If it wasn't their mother, it would be their aunt or someone else that was in charge. The ladies walked around the park in one direction, while the young men walked around in the opposite direction so they could see each other as they passed. If one would look carefully, you could see the young lady pass a note over to the young man as he passed her, and sometimes you might see a young man pass a note over to the young lady. That way they got to know each other. Then when things got a little "thicker" and they knew each other better, they had other privileges. Sometimes they were allowed to stop and talk to each other, but still under the control of some older person. Then when they were ready to marry, the young man would find someone to ask for the hand of this young lady.

Once I did this for a young man. It was on the coast. I had been visiting a little village for some time, taking the gospel there. This young man got saved. Where I happened to be staying there were two young ladies. One of these young ladies had received Christ as her Savior, and this young man came to me and asked if I would go ask for her hand for him. This I did. However, the father did not consent to such a thing. He knew this young man too well. That was the trouble. He said to me, "No. Today, no. Tomorrow no. And, never." He said, "That young man is no use. He goes about, and he carries his possessions in a five-cent paper bag." I knew the boy well. He had been working for me, but he was very lazy. "No," the father emphasized, "I wouldn't see my daughter go in the hands of such a boy as that." So I had to tell this young man that there was no hope, that he had better look elsewhere. That was the way things were done then.

Tegucigalpa is divided by the river. There's just one bridge. Over the bridge you come to the better part of the city. That is where the government made their headquarters. That is where the president has his house.

We had quite a time up in Tegucigalpa, learning many things but, of course, the most important thing we wanted to find out was how to get to the Mosquito District.

We found out that the Mosquito District was practically unknown. The authorities told me I'd have to take a baronesa to go quite a ways further, and then inland. After that, we would have to make our own way by mule. No one knew much about the Mosquito District. The country wasn't opened up yet. Even those in power weren't familiar with the area. After spending some time in Tegucigalpa we thought we'd better make our way back home again to the coast. We went on to Siguatepeque again, spent the night there, and then were up in the morning to get to San Pedro Sula.

# CHAPTER 16: Riding With Bananas to Trujillo

Back again in San Pedro Sula, we saw clearly that if we wanted to find out anything about the Mosquito District, we would have to go to Trujillo. Trujillo was the place that Columbus had landed on one of his voyages, a very old place, indeed. After some little time in San Pedro Sula, my wife and I started out for Trujillo, situated on the Caribbean Coast near Nicaragua. We left our little girl in the hands of Doña Evelena, Mrs. Hockings. Off we started on a rather interesting trip. We left San Pedro Sula on the train and went back halfway to Puerto Cortes where we got off the train and into little boats. They took us up river through canals into another river and then we got off at a place where we met another train, a banana train. We passed through banana towns. As we went, we had the joy of passing out gospel tracts through the window. People would come running and we tried to pass out as many tracts as there were people. They all ran back to their homes, reading these tracts. That was one of the first stages in the work. We went on and on passing through more banana camps. On we went through Baracoa and then La Punta. Those were places where the trains met.

At kilometer 15, there was a factory. The company was experimenting with African palms (*palmeras*). They got a little nut from these palms which they crushed down and eventually made into oil. This oil was used for many purposes: making margarine, soap and other things. Kilometer 15 means the camp was 15 kilometers from the coastal town of Tela. At kilometer 7 was the United Fruit Company dairy farm. They had hundreds of cows there to provide milk for all their workers.

Then we arrived in Tela. Tela is also divided in two. There was Tela Nuevo and Tela Viejo. Tela Nuevo means New Tela. Tela Viejo means Old Tela. That's where the company had its head-quarters. All the bookkeeping was taken care of in Tela, so at that time there were quite a number of Americans living there. They had a port there, of course, where all the bananas were loaded on boats for the United States. There is a river that runs between the two towns. They had a very good bridge over the river so there was no difficulty in commuting between Tela Nuevo and Tela Viejo. Tela Viejo was where people who were not connected with the company lived. Tela Nuevo had special houses for all United Fruit Company workers.

We left the train in Tela Nuevo. The train then went on to Tela Viejo, which was only five minutes further on. We got in about four o'clock in the afternoon. We had left at seven o'clock in the morning to travel the 60 miles or so. We had been asked by Don Alfredo to look for a man who lived there. This man was con-nected with the company. In fact, he was an engineer on the railroad and had been driving the very train we had been on. He invited us to go to his home which was supplied by the com-pany in Tela Nuevo. He was about the only Christian that Don Alfredo knew in Tela. He had contacted him some time before and this dear man had professed to be saved. He did not know very much about him or his life since then. Thank the Lord, he had been going on in a rather Godly way. We soon found out that he was much interested in spiritual things. When we left the train, he directed us to his home.

It was not very comfortable, according to our standards. How-ever, it was all right for us at the present. He had a few children at that time, too, rather small, they were. Small children can make lots of noise so we had plenty of entertainment that night. When he got home from work, he was able to give us more in-formation. We had to take the train the very next morning. To get the train we had to walk up to Tela Viejo, which wasn't very far. We were to take that train to La Ceiba, but this train did not go right into La Ceiba because it was the United Fruit Company train. It only went to a place called Hilame. That was the end of the United Fruit Company territory. The Standard Fruit Com-pany had its own territory that began there.

We were up in the morning, about six o'clock, got on the train, and started off once more. In Hilame, we had to get off and transfer onto the Standard train. The Standard train was a narrow-gauge train. We always had some fun in transferring, as so many passengers were traveling to La Ceiba and other places. These were not really passenger trains; they were banana trains. Any passengers who wanted to make the trip were taken along only as long as they traveled with the bananas. It wasn't very comfortable at times, but one got used to it. There were no alternatives. These trains also carried provisions for the camp commissaries. Those were the company stores that supplied the workers with food and clothing. It takes some time to unload the supplies and then load the empty milk containers. While the train waited, sometimes there was time for us to get off and go to visit the homes of the people to leave gospel tracts. If there was no time, we would just pass tracts out through the window. We used thousands of tracts in those days.

When we got to Hilame, we changed over to the Standard Fruit Company train. On we went on that train, passing through the Standard Fruit Company camps, which were somewhat similar to the United Fruit camps. We enjoyed distributing these tracts through the train window. We also gave them to the passengers sitting in the seats all around us. We went through all the train, of course, and passed out a tract to everyone, which they seemed to enjoy. That's one thing: I very seldom found anyone who'd turn down a gospel tract; in fact, they seemed to be glad to get it.

At last we did reach La Ceiba. La Ceiba is quite a place. It was the Standard Fruit Company's headquarters. It had all its offices there. It had a big commissary there, too. La Ceiba was a banana town much like Tela. There were better houses for those who worked in the offices. At that time, there were lots of Americans there. Later, those Americans left. As Hondurans became more educated and able to take over, more Americans lost their jobs.

When we got to La Ceiba, we did not know anyone there, although Brother Hockings had told us of a man by the name of Zelaya. We promised we'd try to look him up. Zelaya was quite a man. He had been saved years before in Guatemala. He'd been in Puerto Barrios. There had been a mission there holding special meetings. Zelaya went one night to disturb the meetings, had an argument with a preacher, and tried to shut his mouth. Instead, he somehow began to get interested in what the preacher was saying. The Holy Spirit was working on his heart, convicting him of sin. He had been a rather wild character in his youth. As he grew up he had been in trouble with the authorities and everyone else. He realized that night that he was a sinner before God. You know what? He accepted the Lord Jesus Christ that night, and got saved. He turned out to be a wonderful worker and a wonderful man for God.

Don Alfredo had the joy of baptizing Zelaya and his wife when they came to Honduras. Then Zelaya left San Pedro Sula and Don Alfredo lost contact with him, but he had heard he was living in La Ceiba. We promised we would look for Zelaya, which we did. We went to a hotel that night which was not very nice, but it was suitable.

The next morning we started out to see if we could find Zelaya. Eventually we did, after much inquiring. He was well known in certain quarters, as he was so much occupied in the past in Satan's things. Now he was occupied with the Lord's things. He was testifying to the saving power of God. At last we found where he was. He was very happy to see us and to hear news of Don Alfredo and how the work was in San Pedro Sula. Pretty soon, he had us sitting in his home. His dear wife, Doña Maria, had some good strong black coffee ready. There were some black beans and rice and tortillas. We had a satisfying meal there. Of course, we had been speaking to him about our mission and how we were on our way to Trujillo and wanted to see the Mosquito District. He was very helpful, indeed. He gave us more information. He put us up for the night. In fact, he gave us a standing invitation. "Why not come to La Ceiba? Why not come and live here?" he said. Though he had not much, it was always for the Lord, he said.

His principal living at that time was making candy. He made the candy out of sugar, put flavoring in it, mixed it up and it was a very tasty little tidbit when he had finished with it. He made pounds upon pounds of it. When he had 50 or a 100 pounds made, he would sell it wholesale to the different stores. Then he would sell it in the villages around. He gave us much information about the people in the villages. We found that he was very much occupied for the Lord. He was very anxious that we come and visit him often, if not to stay permanently. We had a wonderful time with him. Then we had to go on our way to Trujillo, so we said goodbye to him for now.

The train that would take us to the Aguan River started off at about 6 a.m. That was as far as the Standard Fruit Company's train went. We passed through more banana camps. At last, we came to the Aguan River. That was the first time that we had been there. We had to cross the river in a little boat. They poled you up the river a little way, then the boat came down with the current of the river. Eventually it made its way over to the far side. Then we had to walk about 10 or 15 minutes up to a little village called Sava. We had to look for someone to carry our grips. There were plenty of boys to do that. They would see that you were *gringos* (Americans), as they called us. They thought all Americans had money. They didn't know the difference. They didn't know we were just poor missionaries. Back then we did not have very much money with us. Very little, indeed. Sometimes we were not able to pay what they wanted. In that case, we had to carry the stuff ourselves.

We got to Sava on a Sunday. It was payday. Sunday was a big day there. The little village was crowded with all kinds of people. People from the camps all around had come in. They were selling and buying and everything else. We had to get on our train from there to take us to Trujillo, but we found out there was no train. The train didn't run on Sunday. The trains took a day off for payday, because there was too much killing, too much rioting and it was rather dangerous. Many of the people drank until their money was spent. However, we found a little motel where we could sleep. The man at the motel was very nice to us. He made us as comfortable as could be. We had a little walk around the village and distributed gospel tracts. Many times in the future we had the privilege of doing the same thing. Early in the morning Monday, the train came along. It came from Trujillo, and was going to Olanchito. Then after that, it was going to turn and come back to Trujillo again. When it came along we thought we'd get on the train to see what Olanchito was like.

We got on the train and off we went. Very fortunately, we found that the conductor was an American. He was very friendly. He told us about Olanchito and he also told us that we would have to spend the night there. We got there about midnight and walked around Olanchito and found it an interesting place. We decided to return to see it again some day, which indeed we did. Wonderful work commenced there later on. The next day, we were on our way again, out of Olanchito and passing by Aguan. We passed more and more banana camps all the way. Everywhere you looked there were bananas. We passed out gospel tracts as we went along. We went right on until we came to Puerto Castillo. Puerto Castillo was headquarters for the Trujillo Railroad Company. The Trujillo Railroad Company was owned by the United Fruit Company. It was quite a place. There were cement and brick buildings there. They had a big hospital and a school for the children of the Americans. At that time, there were lots of Americans living there, although most didn't like it because it wasn't very healthful. They had their houses fixed up as comfortable as possible. There was also a commissary there where you could buy most everything that was necessary in that part of the world.

Trujillo is right across the bay from Puerto Castillo. There was a nice view as you went along the water's edge. We eventually reached Jericho. Jericho was where the United Fruit Company kept more cows for milk and meat for their workers. We got off the train in Trujillo at about six o'clock and spent the night in a motel. The next morning we were up bright and early to see what Trujillo was like. Trujillo has two parts as well. It has what they call Rio Negro (Black River), that's the part right down on the sea. Then you go up a hill to get into Trujillo proper. Trujillo is where Columbus first landed on the mainland. It's one of the oldest places on the continent. When Columbus' party got there, they put up some buildings. An old church there has the year 1502 marked at the top of it, but the year fourteen hundred and something is written down below. That's when Columbus landed there, but the church wasn't completed until 1502. It's a Roman Catholic church, of course. Some old ruins of other buildings are still there. The church was still in use. They had their old cannons there, quite a few of them. It was an impressive scene to see the 21 shots going off when some dignitary came to visit. Trujillo was the military headquarters for that part of the country. They had an army barracks there and kept soldiers there. The commander in chief lived there.

There is a gravestone of an American Soldier named William Walker in Trujillo. William Walker was a soldier of fortune. He almost conquered all of Central America. Had he done so, that land would have been part of the United States, but he failed. When he got to Trujillo, he met his Waterloo. He was shot by a firing squad. The marker has been erected in the memory of that man.

One day we met an American. He happened to be a doctor. He lived right in the center of the town. He had been living there for some time. He was living alone. It appeared that he had his home in the United States, but he couldn't live well in the United States for one strange reason; it was impossible, he said, to find liquor in the States without running great risks and paying good money for it. There was no obstacle like that in Trujillo. You could find it all the time and pretty cheap. That was the reason, he told us, that he was living there. He practiced medicine for a short time. He seemed to be a pretty straight, clean man. There was only one drawback in his life: He couldn't live without liquor. However, he invited us up to his home. He had plenty of room, he said. He told us to bring our baggage with us and stay a few days there with him. This we were very happy to do so we could spend a little time in Trujillo to see what things were like and inquire about other things. We made ourselves pretty comfortable there for a few days. I walked around the place and passed out the gospel tracts to people, and found they were very friendly. We found that Trujillo, in some ways, was a little cooler than other places. In fact, there was a little breeze blowing every day.

We started to inquire about the Mosquito District and how we could get to it. We were told it was through Trujillo that we could get to the Mosquito District. We found a very interesting gentleman down in the railroad's office. He was an American, too. He was able to give us more information than anyone else. "Yes," he said, "you can get to the Mosquito District from here." There were two ways to go, but the best way was by boat. If not by boat, we could go by train to Seco. That was the end of the line. When we got off the train, we'd have to make arrangements to hire a guide and someone to carry our baggage, which, of course, we'd have to find out for ourselves when we got to Seco. It would be rather difficult. Then we got into contact with those who knew something more about the boats. We found one man who owned a boat. He told us that he took his boat down there once in awhile, and that he'd be very happy to take me down the coast any time they were going. We just weren't ready. The big thing at the moment was seeing what Trujillo was like. However, I thought that we would try and make that trip to the Mosquito District some time in the future. I'd seen enough of the land to understand that there was great need there. There were no missionaries or gospel work being done in any place that we had passed through on the trip to Trujillo, not since we had left San Pedro Sula.

The time came that we had to leave Trujillo, and we made our way back again in the same way on the railroad to Sava. That's the place that you cross the river to get the Standard Fruit Company train. The train that ran from Trujillo to Sava went through Olanchito as we have already seen. Then we passed La Ceiba

again, and were happy to visit Brother Zelaya, and then on to
Tela. The trip to La Ceiba from Trujillo was a day's journey, and
from La Ceiba to Tela was another day's journey. Finally, we
made our way back to San Pedro Sula, to Mr. and Mrs.
Hocking's place once more.

On the trip it had become clear that in those wide open fields
between San Pedro Sula, Tela and La Ceiba and then right on
through to Trujillo, there was plenty of work to be done. We had
decided that it would be good to go and live in Trujillo and work
from that end, and we had, of course, the Mosquito District further on. We learned later on about the Sambo Indians, and that
there was a big colony of Carib Indians living in Trujillo as well.
They lived right on down along the coast to the border of Nicaragua.

# CHAPTER 17: A Revolutionary Welcome and New Haunted Home

When we got back to San Pedro Sula, we had received a letter from a young man named Allen Ferguson and his wife saying they wished to come down and help us. We wrote back to him and told him there was lots of work to be done. If the Lord had called them to come and join us, we would be very happy to have them. We received a letter back saying that they were coming. We waited, and eventually they advised us when they would arrive in Puerto Cortes. They, too, were coming by boat. We went down to Puerto Cortes to meet them, Don Alfredo Hockings and myself. It was early in the morning when they arrived. I got the dear lady, who had two children, on to the train and brought them up to San Pedro Sula while Don Alfredo waited to help the young man with the baggage. In that way, we were able to avoid the bad experience with customs that Nettie and I had when we first arrived in Puerto Cortes. Then, the next day or two after, Don Alfredo arrived with the young man and his bags. After talking things over, Allen and I decided to take a journey to Trujillo to let him see for himself what the ground was like.

We got on the train in the morning, bright and early of course, to go down to meet the other train going to Tela, but there were quite a number of people on the train. It was packed in. We could hardly find a seat, then Allen shouted to me, "I've lost my wallet!" I'm not sure whether we had advised him to be careful or he would lose his wallet, money, papers and everything else to a thief, but that's just what happened to him. I was in a seat, and I put my head out through the window and shouted at the top of my voice, "Thief. Thief. He's got our wallet. He's inside here somewhere. Police, come." Pretty soon a hand went up and said, "Is this the wallet that was lost? I found it lying here."

Whether that man actually did find it and not steal it is another thing, but there the wallet was with all the money and all the papers in it. That young man learned a lesson – a lesson he was never to forget. In the future, we were always alert to keep our wallets in a place where a thief would have difficulty finding them.

We arrived in Trujillo, had a look around and decided that it was the place for us. We found a house to rent that would be suitable for the two families to live in. It was between Trujillo and Cristales. Cristales was a Carib Indian village. The Carib Indians are an interesting people, as we shall see. We rented the house and made arrangements to move in in two weeks. Soon we returned to San Pedro Sula again.

In the meantime, we went down to Puerto Cortes along with brother Hockings to see about some meetings there. While we were there a revolution broke out. We were unable to return again to San Pedro Sula for some time. We had left Nettie, our daughter Margaret, and this other dear lady with her two children there.

At last we got word that the revolution was over. The railroad opened up again so we could get back to San Pedro Sula. We did not know what to expect, but we knew a number of people had been killed. The rebel party had lost. The government was in control again. When we got to our rented house, we hardly knew the place. There were lots of barricades up. Nettie had stood the test well. She had even put up some barricades of heavy blankets and rugs. She made a place for Margaret in the wardrobe trunk by taking out some of the drawers. The wardrobe trunk was good and strong. Then she got some heavy cord and tied up some blankets to the ceiling and let them hang down. The idea was that if a bullet came into the house it would strike those blankets and lose its power. We were thankful to find that they were all right. They had come through the ordeal well, just a little shaken up, a little frightened. There had been days when it was impossible to buy food. Thank the Lord they had all that was necessary.

We got things fixed up again, but were more excited about going to Trujillo. We had lots to do to get ready. We began to make the necessary arrangements. We had some furniture, trunks, boxes and several other things to go with us so we decided instead of taking the train that we would go by boat. We found a boat going from Puerto Cortes right through to Trujillo and booked passage on it. We loaded our belongings on board and left Puerto Cortes at night. It was nice sailing at first, but a storm came up, not altogether a hurricane, but almost. The wind, the sea, the rain were all coming at once. The boat was being tossed about. Some of us were seasick.

The rough sea didn't get me sick, but I got sick anyway. We had to lie in our bunks most of the time. Our bunks were very small and not very comfortable and our little girl Margaret was up in the bunk above me playing. And what did she do? She jumped on top of my stomach. That acted like a pump and up came the contents of my stomach.

When we sailed near La Ceiba, the captain informed us that he could not stay in port there to wait out the storm. He was going instead to one of the islands off the coast of Honduras. We would stay there until the storm was over. How long would that be, we asked him? He couldn't say, but it would probably be over two weeks before he could get to Trujillo. "But," he said, "if you like we'll land you in La Ceiba and there you can go by train to Trujillo." That's what we decided to do, but it was quite an ordeal.

We were in La Ceiba early in the morning. There were no facilities to land so small a boat there. Passengers had to make the trip to the dock by ladder, but the ladder wouldn't stay in place. It wasn't really the ladder's fault; it was the sea that wouldn't stay in place. Sometimes you were way up at the top near the dock, other times you were way, way down, according to the swells. The sailors explained the procedure to get off the boat. One sailor would get off first. He knew how to do it. He was to grip the iron ladder with his hands as one of the other sailors down below threw the children up to this dear man who would catch them and hand them up to someone else further up the ladder. It was something to see. We got the children up pretty good, then it came to the lady folks. He caught hold of Nettie and, with strong arms, that dear sailor man just walked up the rungs until the other dear man at the top got hold of her. That was the way that we landed. Each one of us in our turn. Finally, we were on solid ground in La Ceiba.

And what do you think? Another revolution was on in La Ceiba. There we were like drowned ducks, and I believe the color of our faces had changed to green. We were advised where we could find a motel, not so very far away. We had only our hand baggage because everything else was left in the small boat to go to the islands to wait out the storm. Then one day, perhaps next week or the week after that, the boat, they said, would eventually arrive with the baggage in Trujillo. We got to the motel and, my, were we glad to be there and to get something to eat and drink. We didn't know whether or not we would be able to get any further because of the revolution. We would just have to wait, but you begin to get accustomed to waiting in that part of the world. We spent the night there, and were informed the next day that the train could take us as far as it went. That was, of course, to the river which had to be crossed in a small boat to get to Sava. When we arrived there, we got over the river all right and eventually to a place where we could stay. It wasn't exactly a motel, but they had accommodations anyhow, and they fixed us up. The dear man there was very kind to us. He informed us that the day before there was lots of shooting and a number of people had been killed, and there would be no passenger train. He said he would make us as comfortable as possible and we could just do nothing else but wait and wait and wait.

However, as we were settling down for the night and it was beginning to get dark, we heard a train. We went out to see the train go by. It was a banana train. A big, long heavy banana train. The caboose came in view as the train stopped, and a man in the caboose shouted, "Where's the American Consul? Are you the American Consul?" "No," I said, "I'm not. I wish I were, right now." "Well," he said, "I have orders to lift the American Consul and take him to Trujillo. Where is he?" I assured him that I saw no American Consul and that I came from La Ceiba that day. I convinced him that I wasn't the American Consul, and that the American Consul wasn't there. "Well, where are you going?" he said. "What are you doing on this line?" He was American. So I told him. I told him my wife was here and another gentleman with his wife and two children and our own little girl and we wanted to go to Trujillo. "Bring them out," he said. "Get them on here to the caboose as soon as you can. I can't wait here. I want to get out of this as fast as I can while there's a little peace, at least." We got the families lined up and into the caboose of this train. Allen's family wasn't used to riding cabooses, or a banana train, either. The first thing we knew several were sprawled on the floor. We had to teach them that they had to sit and hold on tight. This wasn't a passenger train; it was a banana train. When you ride a banana train, you have to hold on.

The train went only as far as Puerto Castillo. It would unload
its bananas there. There was a small passenger train that went
on to Trujillo. We stopped in Puerto Castillo late at night, and
were told where we could get a place to sleep. It was pouring
down rain. A good tropical rain could just drench you through
in a few minutes. We got to the door of this place and, being
late at night, the place was all closed up. We knocked and
knocked and knocked and knocked. At last, a gentleman came
to the door. As luck would have it, he also was an American.
We did not know who he was at the time, but we soon got to
know. He informed us that the lady who owned the place
wasn't there, but he was taking charge of things while she was
away and he would be very happy to accommodate us if he
could, but he didn't know how he could because the place was
almost filled up. He invited us in anyhow and got us something
to eat. He brought some bread and condensed milk and poured
it over the bread and, my, were all the children happy to see
that. They ate it with gusto. We had some coffee, too.

Eventually, after making some changes, he told us that he
thought he could fix us up for the night. Although it wasn't
very comfortable, at least we got a good night's rest. This American's name was Mr. Marston. He was convalescing. He was re-
covering after being cut up with a machete (a large, heavy sword
used in Honduras as an all-purpose ax). He had almost lost his
life.

We were up in the morning and off on the train to Trujillo.
When we got to Trujillo, we just had our hand baggage. We
went up to the house that we had already rented. There we
would make ourselves as comfortable as could be, under the circumstances. We left our wives and children in the station there
in Trujillo, while Allen and I went off to see about the house,
but, lo and behold, when we got there we found it was already
occupied. Someone had come along who wanted to rent it and
the landlord had forgotten all about us. That's the natural thing
to do down there in those countries. First come, first served.
There we were with no place to live. As we inquired, we were
told of an empty house not very far away. Perhaps, they said, if
you can find whoever is the owner, you might be able to rent it.
We found the owner. It wasn't much, but with our wives and
children down at the railroad station we thanked the Lord for
this empty house. It was sufficient for the two families, at least
for the time being. We went back down to the station and then,
with the hand baggage, walked up a hill, by the jail and a dis-

tance further on up to the house. Of course, we had no bedding with us. We had only what our grips could hold, but down in the tropics, especially at certain times of the year, you don't need very much bed clothing. There is no extreme cold, although at times there is extreme heat. We did have two cots. The lady folks got them. The children, Allen and I slept well on the floor. We were all right for that night. We found that you didn't need to go hungry there. Vendors came to the door selling tortillas, meats and other things. In the morning we went down and bought pots, pans, a coffee pot and other provisions and made ourselves as comfortable as possible.

Of course, we were waiting for the boat with our belongings. The storm eventually passed by, but no boat. A week passed by, and no boat. Two weeks passed by, and no boat. The third week, the boat came. How happy we were. We went down, made arrangements and got the furniture and the trunks and got things fixed up. You wouldn't call it luxury, but it was quite comfortable for the moment. Thank the Lord we had a roof over our heads, at least.

Then we heard there was another house for rent right down in the center of Trujillo. We had heard that we could get it cheap. We went and investigated and found that that was true. It was an old two-story building, and was pretty strong. The lower level consisted of one big room as you entered, then opened to the dining room and then a kitchen. Upstairs, there were six bedrooms and a bathroom. We saw possibilities. We decided right away that the lower level would be a good place to hold meetings, which indeed proved to be so. Up above, there was plenty of room for the two families. In fact, we could install a second kitchen up there, which we eventually did, but the most wonderful thing of all was the rent.

We could get the whole place for $25 a month, but we soon found out why it was so cheap. The place was haunted. A haunted house didn't rent very well, but that didn't affect us very much. We did have occasion, at times though, to wonder. Anyway, we now had our furniture and our trunks, and moved into that wonderful place.

Because of the revolution, quite a number of soldiers were there in Trujillo. There was an election, and the party that lost didn't want to go out. This was our welcome to Trujillo.

# CHAPTER 18: The Law of the Mosquito Jungle

The soldiers had their headquarters in the schoolhouse right next door to where we were in Trujillo, so I invited them over to have a gospel meeting. I told them there would be no seating accommodations. They came, right enough. We packed about 50 into that room; just standing room and nothing more. We preached Christ's crucifixion to them. They seemed to enjoy it. At least it was a diversion for them from just sitting around all day. We supplied them with plenty of food and gospel tracts. Pretty soon the new government took over without any fighting and we lost our congregation.

Everything seemed to be settling down. There we were in Trujillo with Allen Ferguson, his wife and two children, Nettie, our daughter Margaret and I, in this big house. It was time to settle down to business, too. We had a big territory to work on and we did not know much about it. We would go off on the train in the morning to a camp, get off the train there and distribute tracts. We would return to Trujillo on the train the same day. We spent some considerable time in that kind of work. We traded off going out, me one week and Allen another week. While Allen was out, I was busy in Trujillo going from door to door offering gospel tracts and books of the gospel of Matthew, Mark, Luke and John. We had received quite a supply of literature from the Scripture Gift Mission in London. They were a great help in the work. I spent much time in the Carib Indian village at Cristales. When my time came to go out on the line, I would often go the length of La Ceiba and spend the night there with brother

Zelaya and have a meeting there. During the day I had time enough to visit and distribute tracts in that city.

There was another place by the name of Sonaguera, midway between La Ceiba and Trujillo. We had heard that there might be interest there because brother Zelaya had visited it often. He would go with his candies - take about 50 pounds with him and sell them in the local stores. He distributed gospel tracts also and, in that way, a little interest was piqued. He had been speaking to quite a few. I eventually went out and spent a little time there. Other times I would go out to Olanchito.

Olanchito was a difficult place because of the distance. When you got there, it was the middle of the day so it was very, very hot. I generally went around visiting after getting off the train and having something to eat. We found some people really interested in the gospel, and tried to make arrangements for a place where we could preach. We prayed much about that, and the Lord opened up the way.

There were other places that we spent considerable time looking over. For instance, there was Sava. Allen and I went to Sava to distribute tracts, but there wasn't much light left. We found an old vacant house and inquired if we could rent it so we could have some shelter over our heads during the night, and we did. We had our hammocks with us. We generally carried our hammocks, that way we could sling them up anywhere. Even if you can't find a building, maybe there would be a tree. We hung our hammocks up in that house and were just settling down for the night when my companion shouted. He jumped out of his hammock and landed on the floor. I didn't know what was wrong. I don't suppose he knew much more than I did. You see, there were *Alacranes* there. Alacranes are scorpions. Sometimes they would fall down from the ceiling. There really was no ceiling in the house, just a roof made out of palm leaves. It was thatched with palm leaves in such a way that it kept the rain out pretty good. When the roofs began to get old, though, after three or four years, they'd begin to leak. You'd get the rain showering down on you during the night and would have to shift your bed many times. This particular night, there was something more solid than rain. It came down with quite a bump on his hammock. Of course, an Alacran wouldn't prove to be a very good bed companion, you can be sure of that, and he didn't relish the possibilities, so up he got. He was wise to do so because those things can sting.

I've had experience with that before. When reaching down to get a piece of wood to put on a fire, for example, you had to be very careful. I wasn't careful enough one time. A scorpion gave me an injection right under my finger nail. It was just like getting a carpet tack hammered in with a hammer. The first thing you do naturally is put your finger in your mouth and blow on it. I did that, and for over five minutes ran about in a circle on the floor with that awful pain, because it is an awful pain. After that initial shock, you have to spend some considerable time as the pain decreases. It takes quite a time to go away. Some of those scorpions are worse than others. There are special kinds that are very dangerous, indeed. They've been known to kill people with the sting. At other times, your whole mouth gets numb, and you can hardly speak.

You have to be careful in the morning as well because you never know what you're going to put your foot down on. Another thing is, you've got to have your hammock properly tied. If you don't, the hammock is going to fall and you're going to come down with it. I've had that unpleasant experience, too. It just brings you down with a bop. You rub yourself for quite awhile afterwards. I learned to see to all of these things after a little experience.

That was our life for some time in Trujillo. We were able to hold individual meetings and start regular meetings. I'd been visiting the Carib Indians quite often, and at last we got some wood and made some benches. That's one thing a pioneer had to do. There was no one else to do it so I had to fix up some place for the people to sit. We were able to get some wood and fix them up, and, well, it was better than nothing anyhow. We invited the people to come and, right enough, a few did come. We started then to sing. I'm no singer, but my wife, Allen and his wife Lily could sing well, so in that way we were able to attract people. We got those benches filled through time. I invited them to come back the next Sunday again for another meeting.

During the week we'd go out visiting. There was interest being shown in some of the banana camps. We'd go out there with the gospels or gospel tracts, visit each home, leave one there, and try, if possible, to get into conversation with whoever lived in the house. Soon they got to know us as we came around. There was no difficulty finding a place to talk to a few people at a time because the residences that the banana company put up for them had space down below. The people lived upstairs, about 9 or 10 feet above the ground on top of posts. If a storm would come up or rain would come in the rainy season, there would be plenty of space for the water to collect underneath. I've known people to have to get up onto the very roof of their houses to escape the water. They'd get up in the rafters and take off some of the zinc roofing to climb out onto the roof because the water was getting so high. In that way, they were able to save themselves until a rescue boat could come along and pick them up.

There was no electric light, so we purchased a Coleman brand gasoline lamp. It was quite an attraction in itself because there was no light of any kind in those camps in those days. The light would attract their attention. We would start to sing and pretty soon the people gathered around. They had already made places to sit down below the house. There was good shade and good shelter under there. So, in that way, we had places to hold the meetings without very much trouble.

There were many notable characters whom we came across while living in the Trujillo District. They were mostly Americans who came down from the United States for various reasons, sometimes to escape the law. It was a good place for them to hide. There was Mr. Marston, who, as I mentioned earlier, was cut up in a machete attack. He was quite a character in his younger years, but he was a gentleman and an American. I don't know the circumstances that brought him down to Honduras. He and two other men, an Irishman by the name of Tom Nestor and another American who I never had the pleasure of meeting, got together and staked a piece of ground in no man's land. At the border of the United Fruit Company's land nearest Nicaragua, there was a lot of open ground. These three men thought that they would stake out a piece of this ground, grow bananas, and sell them to the banana company to ship off to the United States. Quite a few people did this already. They bought a large parcel and began to clear it. They built themselves a house first, and fixed things up so that they could at least be a little comfortable. They needed some workmen, and were about to look for them when a band of men arrived near where they had built their little house. They inquired for directions to Puerto Castillo where, they said, they were going to look for work. Marston and Nestor told them they needn't go any further; they could give them work. There was plenty of cleaning up to be done and preparation for the planting of the banana bits. Banana bits are the root that the banana trees grow from. They eventually gave employment to this band of men. I'm not sure how many there were.

Because they lived out so far from civilization, it was customary for Mr. Marston or one of the other two men to go and meet the train in Seco. The train came from Puerto Castillo twice a week in those days. They'd order provisions and pick up what had been delivered by the train. On this occasion, it was Tom Nestor's time to go. Tom went, and the train came in, but there were no provisions; nothing came. In ordinary times, he would have waited for the next train to come along in two or three days, but somehow he felt that he ought to get back home again. So he started off to get back. I'm not sure how long it took to do the trip, probably quite a few hours. As he got nearer the camp, he saw something that attracted his attention. He could not make out what it was until he came even closer. As he approached, he saw a man in the path. It was one of his companions, Mr. Marston. He had been wounded, evidently, for he was all bloodied. The blood was flowing from him. Tom Nestor did the best he could for him. He found some tree branches and made a little shelter over his head to block the strong tropical sun that was beaming down so hot. He made Mr. Marston as comfortable as he could.

Then he went for help, but when he got near their camp, he saw there was a goat standing in the doorway. They had bought some goats for the goat milk, but the goat usually didn't stand in the doorway, so Nestor wondered what was wrong. There was no sign of life about. As he got nearer and went to the door, he found his other companion, the other American, dead, cut up with a machete. He had big cuts all over him, and there he lay. Tom did not know what to do. The best thing that he could do, he thought, was to go at once back to Seco and see if he could find any help there. Off he started. He had taken some water back with him so that Mr. Marston could have a drink. In Seco, he advised the authorities what had happened. Arrangements were made for a Red Cross railroad car to come out and take Mr. Marston to the hospital.

After piecing the information together, the authorities figured the men who had been working for Mr. Marston and his partners thought that they had money. They took the occasion, when one was gone, to go into the house and see what they could find. They, of course, encountered some little opposition, and the result was that this band of men had killed the American. They also had left Mr. Marston half dead on the path, away from the house. The authorities dug a hole and buried the American, and they got Mr. Marston to the hospital. Infection had started, and maggots had gotten into the wound, but that's what saved his life, so the doctors thought. They had prevented infection. Mr. Marston had to spend considerable time in the hospital.

When we first met him, he was convalescing. He had a little strength back. He had to take life very easily, and we had the pleasure of inviting that dear man up to our home and pointing him to the Savior. He listened very attentively. One remark he made, I have always remembered. "If I thought that," he said, "I do think I would get up on the housetop and with all the power I had, I would advise everyone to come to the Savior." As time went on, we got to know him better. I'd often have long talks with him. He had to give up the banana plantation, but he was a soldier at one time, and had a little pension from that.

After he felt stronger, he made a trip to San Pedro Sula and, while he was walking along the streets, he came across an "ex-wife." He had married her years ago, but for some reason or other they had separated. They had never divorced. She was happy to see him and they were together once more. That dear woman was quite a help to him in his weakness. Eventually, that dear man received Christ as his Savior, and he attended the meetings in San Pedro Sula often while he was living there. Then, as time went on, he got weaker and went home to be with the Lord, which indeed was much better.

His partner, Tom Nestor was now the only one left of the three to look after the banana plantation. He hired a younger man to help in the housework, especially to cook and such things, while Tom was busy supervising the plantation. On one occasion, Tom Nestor went out to do some hunting. He shot an animal and brought it back to camp about two o'clock in the morning. He woke up this young man and told him to get up and dress the animal. He said, "Yes, I'll do that all right," and he went and got the machete. Tom Nestor felt something very hot on his two legs, and here was this young man with the machete slicing at his legs, his arms, his face, all over. He left Tom half dead. In fact, I think the young man thought he had killed him. He fled, and there was Tom Nestor, left all alone in this lonely place, the blood flowing from his wounds. He had sense enough to pull a bucket of water over near where he was lying. This is what kept him alive.

He got the bed mattress, pulled out the stuffing and stuffed the wounds with it. He lay there practically unconscious, and unable to do anymore for himself. The only hope that he had was that he'd made arrangements for someone to come to see about a pig he had for sale. This man was to come in two days time. As he lay there suffering, stuffing the old mattress stuffing in his wounds, having a sip of water once in awhile, he kept himself alive. Eventually, this man came about the pig. When he saw the conditions of things, he traveled to Seco to summon help, and eventually they got old Tom Nestor into the company hospital in Puerto Castillo. He lay there for the longest time. The doctors did what they could for him, and finally he was able to get on his feet again with the help of a cane. He was feeble, yet he could get about from place to place fairly well.

That was his condition when we first met him. He was an Irishman, an Irish Roman Catholic. They can be the hardest ones to penetrate with the gospel. You can hardly touch them at all. They have their own religion. About my wife, he said once, she'd be the best woman in the world, a wonderful woman, if it weren't for her religion. Tom had been a good friend of the company's so it had made financial arrangements to take care of him until the day of his death. He lived for several years. At times, I had the pleasure of meeting with him, speaking with him, but that was about all. There was Mr. Marston gone. There was old Tom Nestor gone. And there was the other American gone. That's what happened in that part of the world.

# CHAPTER 19: Pioneering in Trujillo with a Helpmate

Oh, Trujillo, where we spent 10 exciting years of our life, while living 52 years in Central America. Never a dull moment, ah, yes, that was Trujillo. The very thought of that place brings to mind many very pleasant memories, and yet, at the same time, some not so pleasant. Trujillo, where the bullets from a soldier's rifle came down on the very spot where our two girls and some of their companions had been playing but a moment before. Trujillo, where I wrestled with a man to keep him from killing his daughter who had disgraced him, while my wife ran, got to his bed, pulled up the mattress, grabbed the revolver and ran away with it so that he could not use it. Yes, Trujillo, that place that we can never forget. And thank the Lord, much work was done for eternity in that same place. Yes, Trujillo, that was the place where we were much thought of, but before that, we had to prove ourselves.

There's one thing about a pioneer missionary in a place where no other missionaries have been: He must prove himself. He must prove to the people that he is not a rascal. As far as they know, he may be a thief. He may be the worst man living. How would they know? They need proof. Therefore, the missionary must be one who is willing and able to take a very humble place at times. He must prove to those people his work. How else could they expect to put their faith and confidence in what he says? As one man explained to me once, we have been bitten before and we don't want to be deceived again. That was a wise man. Prove yourself, that's the first thing to be done and that's what my wife Nettie and I set out to do in the beginning in Trujillo.

In the coming day, I'm sure of one thing, my wife will have a rich reward in heaven. What's a wife for? A helpmate, but sometimes a helpmate can even do more than the man. My wife started in to prove herself to the people. She walked for six miles for weeks to attend to two poor girls dying with consumption. Nothing could be done for them; remember, there were no doctors there, no nurses, no help. They were doomed. The only thing that could be done was to comfort them with some little nourishing food, some medicine, milk and such things. She walked those six miles for weeks in the early morning about five, after she fed our little baby Margaret, and came back in time again to go on with her housework. That's what attracted the attention of the people. That's what opened their eyes. That's what proved to them that it was real. They would not be deceived. But, of course, that didn't go down well with some folks, especially with the Roman Catholic priest.

He gave quite a sermon one Sunday morning on the very dangerous snake that had come into the community. That was my wife. Yes, she was a terrible woman. She was going to destroy the whole people. The priest had attempted to deceive the people to such an extent that the principal Carib Indians in Cristales, Trujillo's twin city and the Carib Indian's headquarters, all dressed up in their best. They came to the priest and told him plainly that if he ever spoke against us again there would be trouble. They put it in a manner very plain, indeed. As a result there was no more trouble. The next time Nettie made her way to that village she noticed behind her a Carib man, and in the front of her a Carib man. They were taking care of her. Why? Because they told the priest, "Here's a lady that's come among us, and she's helping the poor. She's taking an interest in the sick. She's doing all she can to help them. And, do you know what? She won't even take one cent for what she's doing." Ah, that got them. Yes, the opposition to the gospel was overcome as far as the Carib Indians were concerned.

They received us joyfully, and the news spread far and wide, so that when I entered one of those Carib Indian villages, if I listened attentively, I could hear, "This is Don Juan, Doña Nettie's husband." And that seemed to be the key word. That was the letter of commendation. We were all right. We weren't deceivers. We weren't rascals. We weren't thieves. We weren't there to take their money away from them. And the Lord used his word among those dear people.

Also in Trujillo there were some Arabs. The Arabs were mostly from Palestine. Some of them had gone to a Christian school there, while the British had control of that land. Then laws changed and many of them came over to Central America. They were the business people. They had the big stores and were the merchants. As to the gospel, they didn't seem to know much about it. So there was a little opposition. Sometimes, going through villages, meeting some of those people; well, they didn't give us a hearty welcome. But the Lord came in and opened up the way among them.

There were two or three Arab families living in Trujillo. One of the family members was Doña Florinda. She had started to attend the meetings, but she couldn't understand very well. There's too much sin brought in to the speaking, she felt. There was too much talk of punishment for sin. That kind of talk makes people uncomfortable, but it's something that's very necessary to speak about first of all, and only then lead them to the one who can save them from the punishment of sin. This dear lady and some of her daughters attended the meetings. Sometimes she said she wasn't coming back. She said she didn't understand. Don Juan would read from this book and very quickly turn to another book, she complained. As time went on, some of her family developed a disease, typhoid fever. Three or four of them went down with the fever. There was no doctor or nurse in that city. There were very few who knew anything about medicine. They had only the witch doctors among the Caribs.

When my wife knew that Doña Florinda was in trouble, she went down and visited her. She found out she had no help. The little that she had had run away. They were afraid of that disease. She had a big store to run and a family. So my wife volunteered to help. "How can that be?" Doña Florinda said. "This is a very dangerous disease, very contagious. I don't think that you should do what you want to do." "Never mind that," my wife said. "That's quite all right. The Lord will give me the protection." So right enough, she stayed down there. I can't tell you how many days, but she stayed until they were all out of danger. That's what opened up the door for the gospel among those dear people, the Arabs. Pretty soon all of that large family professed to be saved, and have been going strong for all these years as a wonderful help in the work. The news of Nettie's acts went very far along the way and, at times, I met up with it.

I had occasion to do some business in San Pedro Sula in one of the big stores. When it came time to pay the bill, they said they were giving me 10% to 15% off. "We know what you did to our people in Trujillo," they said. In that way we had advantages, but of course we weren't living for that; we were living for the salvation of souls, and many of those dear people came to the feet of the Lord Jesus Christ, too. One Sunday afternoon, years later, I sat waiting for the meeting when a car drove up. The car stopped. A gentleman and his wife got out. They were big business people in San Pedro Sula. He had a request to make. "What was it?" I asked. Would I please pray for them? They were in difficulties, financially. "We might lose about a half a million dollars," they explained. Many of the Arabs there are millionaires in business. Now they were in difficulties. Would we pray for them? Yes, why not? Sure. So we prayed for them and away they went. Soon after that we got a message that everything had been fixed up. They didn't lose the half-million after all. We do believe that dear lady, too, is on her way to heaven. Not only her, but her sister as well. In these things the Lord opened up the way for a work among those dear Arab people. Trujillo, yes, Trujillo.

In addition to the various tribes of Indians and the Arabs who live in Honduras, there are the people, *Ladinos*, that are a mixture of the Spaniards who came over with Columbus and the native Indians. In Trujillo, some of them think of themselves as a special kind of people, the elite of the country. Are not they the ones who came along with Columbus? Did they not bring the Roman Catholic priests to the country? Did they not have all the important jobs? They looked down upon many of the others. They considered themselves the "higher class." The society people. It was these kinds of people that hindered the gospel even more than the Roman Catholic priests. They used all means, intimidation and threats. If my wife would go near one of their houses, they might have a boiling kettle of water ready to throw down on her. In many ways, they caused much inconvenience. Their children were encouraged to spit upon our children, and did so. That's very difficult for a mother to take, and sometimes it was all I could do to keep my wife from going out and making a scene. We knew it was safer and better to leave this in the hands of God. And God took care of it in a very remarkable way.

The fame of my wife had been all over the place by this time. She had a little idea of how to treat people in illness, and God brought her in that line. One day a father came to our door. He was a Ladino. He asked me, "Do you think that your wife would have the time to leave the wonderful work that she is doing and come to our house to see our child who is very ill?" This little boy, about two or three years of age, had developed some kind of a lump on his head. They had taken him a long way to find a doctor. In fact, they saw two or three doctors but to no avail. That lump seemed to grow. It was inflamed, very angry looking. The poor little fellow was in pain, and his parents were at their wits end. They did not know what to do but, as a last remedy, they thought that it would be better to leave many of their beliefs behind and consult my wife. Yes, she would go, and she went. She looked at his lump and she looked at it again. She lifted up herself in prayer to God to give the needed guidance, help and wisdom. And she started in. I can't tell you all she did. Applied poultices, hot water, bathed it, cleaned it very careful and squeezed it. She kept that up nonstop. Even in the night time she would go back and do the same thing over again for several days. Then, one day, like a boil, it burst open. What do you think came out? Hundreds, now I'm saying hundreds, of little worms. Those little worms were eating into the flesh. Not only to the flesh, but down into the brain. Carefully, she picked those worms up, one after the other, with a little pair of tweezers. Eventually, she got them all out, and then used some kind of disinfectant. She kept going back to that house until that little fellow was all right again. After that, there was a change in that community. The Ladino persecution stopped. And, why? Because of Nettie's work. Sad to say, we never did see very much of the Lord's work done with the Ladinos. They were too rich, maybe.

Trujillo, yes, Trujillo, where my wife was tried and tested to almost the breaking point. Of course, these tests occur at times in nearly every missionary's experience. Our barrel of meal, our staple, had been nearly empty for some time and we could afford no more meal to put back into it. The flagon of oil was going down, too. On this particular day, I was going out to visit an Englishman. He lived out along the railroad line and he had a banana farm. I said goodbye to Nettie at about five in the morning: "To start off," I said, "I am going to a place where I know there'll be plenty to eat, but I'm afraid you're not going to have much." "Well, that's all right," she said. "We'll fix up somehow." At that time, we also had a young man, his wife and two children living with us temporarily, in addition to Nettie and our daughters, Margaret and Johnette. I went on my trip and had plenty to eat. But when Nettie got to the meal barrel, it was even lower than she had thought. In fact, she couldn't scrape a crumb out of it. As to the oil, it was down to the last few drops. What to do?

She got angry, angry with the Lord. She fought it out with Him, so she said afterward. "Didn't you tell us we would come down here and you would look after us? Didn't we understand that all we would have to do is to spread the good news of salvation, and everything would be taken care of? Well, where is that care now? There's nothing in the house. Here are these two children in their own little beds. What about them? Are they going to starve? There must be something wrong. What is it?" She got quite excited about it, naturally. She decided to write a letter to her father. She thought that she would tell him what was happening. "But, no. Oh, no," she told herself. "That's not trusting the Lord." So she did not write the letter. Shortly, there was a knock on the door. It was the mail boy. That was very strange. It wasn't mail day. The mail wasn't supposed to come on that day. However, there was the mail boy. He held out a letter and he said, "Doña Nettie, is this yours?" She looked at it, and said, "Yes, it is." That letter had been all over Honduras for two weeks. There was the mark of the American Consul on it. There was the mark of the British Consul on it. There was the mark of the United Fruit Company on it. There was the government of Honduras' mark on it. And finally it was here. The mail boy said, "Yes, I knew it was yours."

She opened the letter and out came 10 pounds. When she saw that 10 pounds, she rushed off to have it changed. Even though there was no bank in that place, some of the merchants were very glad to get British pounds. Very soon she had it changed to lempiras (Honduran currency), and off she ran before the meat market was closed. You see, there was no refrigeration and the meat market closed as soon as the beef was sold. They just slaughtered enough for the day and no more. She ran to see if there was any meat left and, sure enough, there was. Then she ran and got some vegetables and pretty soon there was a big pot of soup. She dished it out to that dear sister, her two children and our little girls. After she served them, she started to serve herself, but couldn't. She couldn't. She had to excuse herself, go to the bedroom, get down on her knees and ask pardon from the Lord for ever doubting him and his power to supply that which was needed. So there it was. And, I might say, the Englishman got saved, too. That was something bright. Without sacrifice, you know, there's nothing.

Thank the Lord for his provision all the way along. Yes, God provides. If he calls, if he sends, then he must provide as needed. He provides sometimes in different ways, sometimes in remarkable ways. Sometimes he's providing and you don't even know it. There was one thing that troubled me before even going into the mission field. I knew I would never be able to look after my family the way others do. What about the children? I never would be able to give them the education that others give. What about when the time comes for them to be married? Where will the money come from? That's what worried me more than anything else, but we just had to trust the Lord.

Nettie's father was a very remarkable man, a very good man, a man full of wisdom. He began to write and inquire about conditions in Trujillo. He asked about the place in which we were living. He asked about the housing problem. He asked about prices. He asked if there were houses for sale. Of course, in letters we tried to answer his questions. Eventually he wrote to say he was sending a check to buy a certain house. The only thing, he said, it must be for the children, not for us. That's what he did. That house was for them. It was not for me or my wife, nor even for the work, it was for the children. That was way back in the '30s, but, you see, he was looking way forward to the '50s. That was rather much for me; however, that's how it was. The house was bought in their names. It was one of the old ones. The walls were 18 to 24 inches thick. It was a good solid house. It needed a little repair, of course, but it had been added on to so it could fit two families. We moved into it, and we rented the house from our children. That was funny, but it was a fact. We might as well be giving them the money as some stranger. Part of the house was divided and we were able to rent that portion. That rent paid for the repairs of the main house. Then afterward the rent and money from the sale of the house went also into the account of the children. When it came time for them to be educated and married, the money was there. That's how it was done. We had nothing at all to do with it. It was the Lord's doings. Many wondered how we got the money to finance our daughter's educations and marriages. It was the Lord that did it. He opened up the way for it. The money was theirs, it was not ours. Many times we could have used it, it's true, but when I was a little boy I was taught that I shouldn't tell lies and I shouldn't steal. My wife was taught the same thing. We were very, very careful not to take any of that money. It wasn't ours. It would have been stealing. We kept it separate from our own money.

As you know by this time, my wife excelled in many things, and she provided two wonderful daughters and the pioneering breakthrough we needed to get accepted by the people (Caribs, Arabs and high society) and started on the Lord's work in Trujillo.

(Clockwise) John's grandfather Joe Ruddock, a visitor, John's father holding him, and John's mother holding John's brother Hugh in front of John's birth-home in Growel, Northern Ireland.

John as a mischievous young man.

A young Nettie in Scotland.

John handing out tracts in 1923 with gusto to the "precious" Mexican children in East Los Angeles.

John and Nettie's wedding day in Pasadena, California, with John's mother and father.

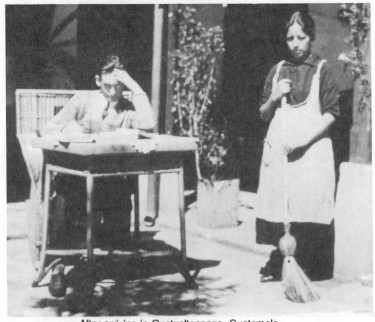

After arriving in Quetzaltenango, Guatemala, John and Nettie set about learning Spanish.

Nettie – learning Spanish

John speaking with Assembly elders in 1928.

The aftermath of a Guatemalan volcano eruption where John administered to the victims' souls.

John's Guatemalan home-away-from-home.

A typical Quetzaltenango street.

Don Alfredo Hockings fit out as colporteur

Don Alfredo Hockings performing one of many river baptisms.

Don Juan and Don Alfredo, pioneer missionaries, posing at a Carib residence near Trujillo, Honduras.

Nettie with Margaret (left) and Johnette in arms in front of haunted Trujillo house where revolutionary soldiers attended first service.

First Carib to come to the Lord stands near an early gospel hall.

Nettie's parents, Dugald and Jean Baird.

Dugald purchased the Trujillo home below and had John pay rent to Margaret and Johnette.

This portion of the house was built by a contingent left after a Christopher Columbus voyage. It fronts the park where the Carib boy heard John 3:16.

Dona Florinda (right) (and her mother), who Nettie nursed to health from typhoid fever to win over the Arab community.

Ex-atheist Mariana (front right) took the good news back to her village.

John and Nettie paddling cayucos up the Mosquito Coast's Patuc River.

Nettie and a Carib pose at a William Pitt settlement grave discovered in Mosquitia.

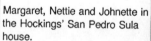

Margaret, Nettie and Johnette in the Hockings' San Pedro Sula house.

Alan and Lily Ferguson, children and a Carib in Trujillo

A missionary family portrait: John, Nettie, Margaret and Johnette.

Waiting for a banana train, like the one shown on the next page, with banana trees behind.

Banana Train

An old style chapel in Santa Rita.

Leading a procession of believers
to another river baptism.

Carib boys playing in the Mosquito Coast surf.

The Carib assembly in Cristales on the edge of the Mosquito jungle.

The first Honduran gospel hall in San Pedro Sula.

In sunglasses, the general who appointed John bishop of the Mosquito District.

Before and after shots of the Tela Gospel Hall built by John.

Shots during and after construction of their house in Tela.
Johnette in front with the builder John.

The view of Tela to the Caribbean from the house.

Johnette and Nettie, with her grandson, the co-author, on a Jeep in Los Angeles.

John and Nettie with the co-author at three months in Honduras in 1954.

Nettie and John in a tranquil pose in 1964.

The old folks home under construction in 1972. John dedicated this wall to his mother who lived to 103.

John and Nettie, center, with their old folks in 1978.

# CHAPTER 20: A Trip into the Mosquito Jungle

## Notes on a trip to the Mosquito District:

**30th April 1934**

**1:30 p.m.** Received a message that a boat would leave for Patuca River, Mosquito District, the following day. Had waited for this message for three weeks.

**3 p.m.** Captain of the boat paid us a visit and kindly gave me some valuable information as to traveling necessities, etc. He is going up to hunt for alligators and, as he intends on going up the river quite a distance, it will give me a good start.

**1st May.** Waiting on boat but it will not arrive until tomorrow.

**2nd May.** Still waiting on boat.

**3rd May.** An American explorer paid us a visit this a.m. He hopes to leave for Mosquito District soon, and he would like me to go with him. He is looking for the lost white city and I for lost black sinners. His is some job; he will win earthly fame if he finds the city, and it will surely be earned, as he will have days and days of hardships before him. He had already been out but had to return owing to an attack of dysentery. For two cents, he would return back to the States, he says. When men of the world will put up with days of hardships to find lost cities, why cannot we for lost souls?

**2:30 p.m.** Received notice that boat will leave at 6 p.m. so I must get my things down.

**7:45 p.m.** We are off. Sea is a little rough.

**10 p.m.** Stop and drop anchor. Captain decides to wait in bay until sea gets calmer. Passengers lie down on the deck to sleep and I do the same. Three or four hours later we start off again and get out into open sea, which is a little rough.

**Friday 4th**

**5:30 a.m.** We get up. It does not take long to dress as we did not undress. It is a beautiful morning. Sea is calm.

**6:30 a.m.** Breakfast of coffee, bread and fish. Good. All morning we have been passing Carib villages, some of them I have visited with tracts before and others, no.

**6 p.m.** Arrived at mouth of Brus Lagoon. Should have arrived at 2 p.m., but wind was against us and sea was rough. Dropped anchor and spent the night inside lagoon on the boat.

**Saturday 5th.** There was engine trouble, and we did not get away until late. Arrived Brus Lagoon Pueblo about noon. Captain kindly took me to the home of a man who is half American and half Indian. I believe he is saved. He was saved through the preaching of the gospel by a Moravian missionary who has worked in Nicaragua among the Indians there. There is now a Moravian missionary in Honduras. He moved over the border from Nicaragua recently to work among the Indians of the Mosquito District. One of their local preachers is expected here tomorrow. He is going to live here and preach the gospel. This man with whom I have stayed just knows he is saved and that is all. I spent the evening with him over the Scriptures. He speaks English well. After supper he took me over to another house to sleep. I had a room to myself. In the night I heard something or someone moving about the room, but although I looked around with the aid of my torch could see nothing. All was quiet for a time, then the noise began again. I switched the torch on just as something opened the door with a bang and rushed down the steps. From the sound it seemed to be an animal with four feet. Several dogs began to bark. After that I slept well until the morning, when the pigs outside woke me up.

**Sunday 6th.** Indian preacher arrived from Nicaragua during the night, and all the village turned out to see him. He had a meeting in the morning and a Sunday school in the afternoon. Between times I tried to bring the truth of separation before him and also sought to show him the error of infant sprinkling, etc. May the Lord open his eyes to see these precious truths. It is good to see the gospel being preached in this place but sad to see what is being taught.

**Monday 7th 6 a.m.** Am supposed to start upriver this a.m. but do not see the boat yet.

**8 a.m.** Boat has just arrived in bay. Will have to wait until they send small boat for me. There is a nice breeze blowing, which makes it cool. It rained this morning.

**4 p.m.** Am still waiting for small boat to come and get me but it has not arrived so far. This is the land of *mañana*.

**Tuesday 8th. 7:30 a.m.** Boat arrives to take me off. Got into boat pan with outboard motor and leave about 8:30 a.m. Ride up river is very nice at first. The mouth of the river is very wide and there are islands scattered here and there. Pretty soon we leave this behind and both sides of the river are covered with tropical growth. It is green and pleasing to the eye. Varied colored birds are flying around. One kind builds its nest in the high trees, the nests hanging like baskets from the branches. This day is not too hot; a nice breeze is blowing. It seems to disappear for a few minutes and then starts up again.

**3:30 p.m.** We reach the first alligator camp and leave off one bag of salt for salting the skins. Alligators are the business of the party I am traveling with. The Indians hunt the alligators at night with the aid of lights. They harpoon them and then kill them. After that they skin them, salt the skins and store the skins away until the boat pan comes up to get them.

**4 p.m.** We pass a village.

**4:30 p.m.** We reach another alligator camp, leave off salt and go on.

**5:30 p.m.** Reach another camp. Here we make camp for the night, get supper and the mosquitoes chase us to bed. My mosquito net was not made for this kind of mosquito. After killing about 20 and seeing about 50 more appear to see what all the noise and smell was about, as those 20 had already sampled my blood, I gave up the chase and wrapped myself up in my blanket, head and all. Came pretty near to suffocating myself, but, it was better than letting the mosquitoes continue their feast.

**4:30 a.m. Wednesday 9th** Got up and went down to river in the dark to have a wash and shave. After breakfast left with one of the men to walk to an Indian village. After three-quarters of an hour's walk, we reached the village. Pretty soon a crowd gathered to see us, and I told them the story of God's love, the man with me acting as interpreter. We left there and walked to another village where we again told the good news. These poor Indians have not many comforts. Their chief foods being green banana, plantain and yucca. Those who hunt alligators are paid in cloth. The lady of the house where we stopped kindly made us some fried bananas and dried meat. It was a good feast for a hungry man. We arrived back at camp about noon. I bring a headache back with me. On the way back through the first village at which we had stopped, an old lady called us and gave us some dried meat and two plantains. Our boat pan has gone up the river a short distance to deliver salt to a few more camps. Another boat pan is expected, which will take me still further up the river.

**6 p.m.** The boat pan has not yet arrived, so we prepare to go to bed before the mosquitoes get too busy. The captain has kindly given me a new mosquito net, which is suitable for this part. I fixed it up and to my great joy slept well as I was free from my mosquito companions.

**Thursday 10th 6 a.m.** Get up feeling rested and found boat pan waiting to take me further on.

**11 a.m.** Motor boat pan arrives going up to Brighton's camp. They kindly take me along. We passed another village and a few alligator camps on the way. The river is very low at this time of the year, which makes it difficult to travel. Once the outboard motor struck a sunken tree; at another time we ran over a tree trunk that almost capsized the boat. At 3:30 p.m. we arrived. Mr. Brighton made me feel right at home and gave me some valuable information regarding the Indians, etc. Had the opportunity to visit many of the workers in the camp and preach the gospel to them. One mother brought her baby for me to christen. This gave me an opportunity to tell them the truth about this. I do not know if they understood or not, as they just know about the Roman Catholic Church and the others that they have heard about christening the children.

**Friday 11th 4:30 a.m.** Mr. Brighton wakes us up as he kindly offers to take me further up the river in his outdoor motor boat. The boat pan, however, has drifted away downstream in the night, and he had to send someone to look for it. After waiting for several hours, we start off. We pass more alligator-hunting camps. The river banks are pretty. Bananas are growing on both sides. No one remembers these being planted. They seem to have been there for centuries. The river practically divides the soil in two. On one side there is rich soil suitable for growing almost anything. This ground is of course covered by tropical growth. On the other side there is an open country with fine trees growing and lots of grass suitable for cattle. This being the dry season, the river is very low; lots of tree trunks and branches being lodged in its mud. After striking one or two mud bars and being almost capsized, we reach one of Brighton's banana camps. Here we have lunch, after which the motor man decides to have a look at the motor. This took longer than he expected with the result being Mr. Brighton cannot take me any further as it would be too late for him to return home that night. He left me after making arrangements for me to be taken up the river tomorrow by a poling crew. This gave me all the evening in the camp with a good opportunity to preach the gospel. Here everyone goes to bed just after dark (6:30) and gets up just before daylight. I, of course, being here, do the same.

**Saturday 12th 5:45 a.m.** We are off up the river, my poling crew consists of two men and one woman with a baby. The two men stand up and pole while the woman sits behind and guides the boat. Like the woman, I find it more healthful to sit, too, or I am afraid I would soon be sitting in the water. All the canoes and boat pans are made out of solid tree trunks. Some are over 50 feet long and over 4 feet in breadth. I have seen some this length and am told there are some still longer than this.

**9 a.m.** We reach the village and have a look around. I took a picture of a family here. They, of course, had to dress up for the occasion. I bought a stick in this village. They use the stick for stirring their food, which is made from green bananas.

**9:45.** The baby drops its bottle overboard so we spend two minutes fishing for it. We pass the village of Salpatanto.

**10:35 a.m.** Pass another small village. Here lives a man who speaks Spanish. He is from Nicaragua and has lived in these parts for 30 years. He knows the place well and seems to know where the Indians live. He says he would like the missionary to come and live here so that the children might learn to read and write. There are, of course, no schools of any kind in this part of Honduras. The boat has just struck a rock and away goes the *huscal* again. I succeeded in rescuing it this time.

**12 noon.** We reach the first camp belonging to some Germans.

**1 p.m.** Reach another camp. One of them is home and he makes me welcome, and I welcomed two cups of hot coffee. He is busy planting bananas in this section. I spend the evening and the night in this place. I am afraid we broke the law of the land or at least of this part of the country by staying up late and talking well into the night. It is a lonely life living as these men do. They do it for worldly gain. Oh, that there were more obeying the command of the Lord. "Go ye into all the world and preach the gospel to every creature." During the night I heard a noise and was told that a tiger had passed by.

**Sunday 6:30 a.m.** I leave in a canoe that is going still further up the river to the Germans' headquarters.

**9 a.m.** We saw a tapir. The poler took a shot at it but missed. We pass little settlements of Indians who have come over the border from Nicaragua because of the revolutions there. I bought a piece of cloth made from the bark of a tree for a string of beads. At one point the river was so low that we had to get out and push.

**11:30 a.m.** We reached the Germans' headquarters and they were very happy to see a white man, for it is very seldom they see one. These Germans are growing rice and bananas. It is a new venture. They have had their first crop and it was a good one. They told me they hope we will come and work among the Indians as it will be a benefit to them. They say they see the difference in some of the Indians who have come over from Nicaragua and who belonged to the Moravian Mission there. Spent all the evening until 9 p.m. talking to these two men and had a good opportunity to preach the gospel to them. Word had spread that a missionary had arrived, so the Indians came up to look me over. Some of them I was told had poled up river for two hours.

They were disappointed that I could not speak their language. I should have liked to speak to them through an interpreter, but the two Germans had not had an opportunity to speak to a white man for a long time, so they kept me busy talking to them. They were able to give me a little more information and I found out from them that I was at the end of the Sambo country, and it would take two more days poling to get to the Somo tribe. They told me that there were not many in the Somo tribe and that they spoke another language. I feel I have accomplished quite a bit. Since there is an outboard motorboat pan going down river on Monday, I shall take the opportunity and get as far down with it as I can on my return journey. I hope to get to the Plantain River. This is the route taken to look for the lost white city. But I am looking for lost black sinners.

**Monday 14th 5:30 a.m.** We are on our way downstream. The boat pan is large, so we have to float at first as the river is shallow. Pretty soon the motor is humming and we are on our way. Behind us in the distance is the volcano. It is to all appearances dead. Mr. Brighton has been on top of it. It appears to be a limestone rock formation, and although no crater can be seen, the Indians claim to have seen it spit out fire. It was with difficulty Mr. B. got the Indians to go up with him. The devil would be very angry, they said, and they would not return alive. When they got up, a thunderstorm started, and the Indians were sure that it was the devil that was angry. They ran as one man and left Mr. B. alone.

The women folks in the villages below were terribly frightened, too, and came running out to meet their men folks and to give them a helping hand. They were all sure Mr. B. would not return alive. He seemed to be proof against the devil and, to their surprise, returned all safe and sound, having suffered nothing more than a drenching, and the inconvenience of having to carry his things and make a perilous descent. Around the bend in the river, as these folks say, (I think they mean a dozen bends) there is a blind alley, where the waters rush down and whirl around, and to the poor boat crew that would get into it, it would indeed be the "Portal del Infierno."

**2:30 p.m.** We reached a small village and I visited a few houses, one Spanish-speaking woman invited me to take some coffee, which I gladly did. I had coffee and eggs and some kind of bread. I enjoyed it as I was very hungry. Later we stopped at another village and one of the Indians brought me a gift of five eggs. After this we had a little engine trouble and had to spend some time doing repairs. We then made a small camp. Later we reached Brighton's camp where we spent the night.

**Tuesday 15th 6:30 a.m.** We are on our way again downstream. Spent a short time visiting a camp I had visited on the way up. Found an old man pretty sick and preached Christ to him. While sitting in the boat waiting for the rest to come, a father brought his little year-old daughter for me to name. I was glad to help him out, and I gave her the name of Cornelia. This pleased him immensely and I, of course, had to dig down in my grip for a present.

**10 a.m.** We are off again. Made various calls at the different places.

**8 p.m.** Reached Brus Lagoon village safely, although we had to make 1 1/2 hours in the dark. The mouth of the river having so many small islands makes it quite dangerous in the dark. Our boat pan was heavily loaded, so we had to get out and push, the water being just over our knees. At last we had to walk 200 yards carrying our things. Not having had anything to eat all day, I was hungry and enjoyed a meal of cassava bread.

**Wednesday 16th 7 a.m.** After breakfast tried to get someone to take me a little further but could do no more than make arrangements for tomorrow, therefore *mañana* I hope to get on my way again.

**Thursday 17th.** Last night tried to bring before the preacher's wife the necessity of carrying out the Word of God in our lives. She had never heard of celebrating the Lord's Supper the first day of the week. As to baptism, she knew nothing about burying the old man. Sprinkling is the method they use. I tried to persuade one man not to kill another. I found the Indians only work when they need cloth. Just as soon as they get what they want, they go off hunting again or fishing. Theirs is a free and easy life. Naturally, feasting comes after hunting. They are great meat eaters when they can get it. When a deer, a wild pig or a tapir is brought in, they do not stop until all is eaten. On the other hand, they can live for days on banana mixed with coconut oil.

**8:30 a.m.** We are off again – this time in a little canoe. No polers are needed as we are no longer traveling against stream upriver but in the lagoon. One man can manage. He had a square piece of cloth for a sail and we seem to be getting there.

**9 a.m.** We reached the mouth of the lagoon so the man secured his boat away, adjusts my grip suitable to carry, puts my camp bed on his back and by 9:30 a.m. we are walking along the beach. A two-hour walk brings us to Plantain River. I had a good look at it. Two men from the U.S. are there just now suffering hardships to find the lost city, while another, the one who visited us, was driven back by dysentery. Up that river I know there is not only one lost city but many lost souls, yet we are not so keen to go and find them. Here at Plantain River village I had quite a time preaching the gospel. One man there of the Carib tribe told me that he is a Christian. He had traveled quite a bit and heard the gospel and accepted the Lord Jesus. He asked me if I was a Moravian, a Baptist, or a Methodist, or an Adventist.

Upon my saying I was not, he said, "Then what are you?" "I am what the Bible says I am," I replied. I asked him where the Bible said we were to take any of the names he mentioned. "It says we are Baptists," he replied. Handing him my Bible, I asked him to show where the Bible said we were Baptists. After looking a few moments, he said he remembered it was not in the Bible but in another book. I then explained to him that that was going by what men said and not obeying the Word. "I never understood that before," he said. He says he is coming to Trujillo so we trust he will learn how God would have him walk. We had lunch and rested until 1 p.m. Three-quarters-of-an-hour walk brought us to an American's place and, as the sun was hot, we rested until 3 p.m. when we started off again. We met Fred Haller, one of the Germans who owns the place up the Patuca River. He was on his way up there, and having just come from Trujillo, brought me news that all was well at home.

**6:15 p.m.** We reached the village of Cocoville just as darkness was settling and secured a place to put up my camp bed. Of course, no food could be found. This is the great difference between working here and working in the homelands. However, there were plenty of fires in the place so out of my grip came cooking utensils, coffee, hard biscuits, etc., and soon we were enjoying a well-earned meal. After that I had a good opportunity to preach the gospel.

**Friday 18th. 4:30 a.m.** We are off again. This time in another canoe up another lagoon. I am becoming quite an expert canoe traveler. I even washed, shaved and cleaned my teeth while we sailed along.

**6 a.m.** We reached Mrs. Brunner's place and she welcomed us and gave us a hot cup of coffee. While eating, I preached the gospel to her.

**7 a.m.** We are off again and pass a few Indian villages. After we pass Palacios, we come to Carib villages.

**9:30 a.m.** We reach Pati's, and make a call to drink some coconut water. I also took the opportunity to distribute a few tracts and gospels and say a word to those who gathered around.

**10:30 a.m.** At the end of lagoon. We walked a distance to Tocomacho across the sand and on the way passed several Carib villages. The Caribs are increasing in numbers and there is a great need among them. I should have liked to spend more time with them, but not having sufficient gospels with me I decided to return home and go back later. From Tocomacho we again cross another lagoon and rent a canoe in which we travel until we reach a banana plantation owned by a German. Here I parted with my carrier and returned to Brus Lagoon. I spent the evening and night and was entertained by another German, a man of independent means, who has spent four years in solitude seeking truth, the secrets of life and the cause of depression. He claims to have found the answer to all three and has written two articles for the Literary Digest. He is most indignant because he has not seen them published.

I asked him what truth was and he explained that it was body, soul and spirit. He compared life to the pendulum of a clock. The center is the dividing point. When it swings to the left, this is changing from one state to another. If he lives 40 years in the earth, then he is changed and lives 40 years in eternity, either in Heaven or Hell. Then he re-enters the earth in the form of a newborn babe again. I told him I could not believe that until I saw it written in the Word of God, and asked him to show me the passage. First Corinthians 15:50 he replied. "We shall be changed, etc." This, of course, seemed so ridiculous to me that I laughed right out loud. This made him angry and he would not listen to anything I had to say.

**Saturday 19th.** Have secured another carrier so we start off by canoe. One-and-a-half hours brings us to the end of the lagoon. We then walk to the railroad track. This walk developed into a rather long one as the carrier lost his way and we had to go through jungle and thick bush until we found it again.

**11 a.m.** We reached the railroad track and my carrier returned home.

**12:45 p.m.** The train came along and I boarded her.

**9 p.m.** Saw me in Trujillo tired but happy to have returned safely and full of thanksgiving to God for all His mercies by the way.

John Ruddock
Trujillo, Republica de Honduras
Central America
30th April, 1934

# CHAPTER 21: Sowing Seeds in Banana Fields

The work among the Carib Indians or the Morenos, as they were sometimes called, was rather slow. Indeed, it was three years before we saw a movement. I never will forget the day that a middle-aged Carib Indian man came up to the house to tell us that he had received the Lord Jesus Christ as his Savior. That was indeed a very joyful day. Not long after that, another man professed to be saved.

Shortly after, a young man came to the door, introduced himself and told us that his father had sent him up. His father was the second Carib Indian to profess to be saved. This young man of 21 years of age had heart disease. He couldn't lie down. He was forced to sit up at all times. His father had taken him to a hospital where doctors examined him and told him that he had a very short time to live. So his father was very anxious that he should hear the gospel. He explained that to me, and I spent some considerable time speaking to that young man and before he passed away, he too professed to be saved.

About that same time, we were working a lot among the children. The children, of course, in my younger days were my specialty. We were able to buy a little place in Rio Cristales, a Carib Indian village near Trujillo, for 40 dollars. It wasn't very large, but we were able to pack about 100 children in that little room. At the same time, we had the Sunday school going in Trujillo. That was two Sunday schools in one day, as well as the preaching of the gospel in Trujillo on Sunday nights.

During the week I went out to the villages and banana camps. One day two young men came to the door. They asked for Don Juan. They explained that they had come from Aguan, a Carib Indian village that was about a day's journey from Trujillo. Their father had sent them. Evidently, he had lived at one time in British Honduras (now Belize) and there he had heard a little of the gospel, but it was tainted with Seventh-Day Adventist teachings. He was a little confused. Would I be kind enough to pay him a visit in Aguan? he asked. "With great pleasure," I told these two young men. They asked me when I could leave. They explained that they would have to make travel arrangements. There was no road. Travel was only possible by foot or on mule back and canoe.

In two days, I started off with them. In such trips into the jungle, 2:00 or 2:30 in the morning is the time to start. We walked about seven minutes down to the beach. There they had a canoe ready. They paddled along the shoreline until we came to the entrance of Guaimoreto Lagoon. We went underneath a railroad bridge and on right to the lagoon.

They told me that I'd better keep my hands inside, not to hold onto the side of the canoe because there might be water snakes. Soon daybreak began to overtake us. These two men were handling the canoe so I didn't need to occupy myself with that. We had started off so early in the morning that I hadn't shaved. Riding in a canoe is soft going, so I started in and finished shaving. It's not like on a bus or a truck where you're bouncing all over the place. It was enjoyable. About 2 1/2 to three hours through that lake there was a little wind, so we put up the sail to go a little quicker. At last we came to Barranca, a village with a few houses. Carib Indians living there had the mules ready.

I always travel light for myself, but very heavy for the Lord. I had lots of gospels, gospel tracts, Bibles and such things. One mule took charge of it, and another mule, well, I got onto the back of that mule. If you have never traveled by mule back down there, you have a few things to learn. You're supposed to sit on the top of the mule, but sometimes you find yourself underneath the mule. Have a good look at the saddle and see that it's tied properly. As you go along, maybe the mule will get hungry. If you happen to have a straw hat on, look out. I've seen a mule turn around and snap the hat from the head of one of our sisters and begin to eat. The poor sister had to put up with the sun that day.

Leaving Barranca, there are two ways to go. The nearer way is to go through a marshy part of land. I once traveled through there when the mosquitoes were so thick that I didn't know what to do. After praying to the Lord and asking for help, a bee came along and took charge of the mosquitoes. Now, however, it is just after the rainy season and that path is flooded, so we went down directly to the beach to travel along the sand. That, to me, was a very joyful trip. Along the water's edge the sand is hard, but more inland it is very soft, very difficult to walk in. However, this time I was on the mule, so I didn't mind.

After two hours, we came to what they call Las Tres Cocos, that's three coconut trees together. That's always a very pleasant place to stop. Up the trees the Carib Indians went and brought down several coconuts for coconut water. In another two hours, we came near Aguan. The villagers knew, of course, that we were coming, so out they came to meet us, quite a number. They helped us get to Aguan Village. There we met that dear old man. I've forgotten his name.

I didn't put a number on him. That's the only way I could remember names in the camps. I'd put a number on each boy or girl, number one, two, three, four, five, six, seven and so on. I would look at them if they were misbehaving and I would say, "number six." Whoever that was. I never could remember names.

However, this dear man was waiting on us, but I had told these two young men that the first night I would like to have a rest. I would likely arrive with a migraine headache, which was my thorn in the flesh, and I wouldn't be capable of even thinking straight. I got a place to myself and was able to get a good night's rest. A good night's rest is something to be thankful for.

The next day I had the privilege of speaking to this dear man who had sent for me. He told me something about his past life. He had lived in British Honduras, so he could speak a little English. He had come into contact with the Seventh-Day Adventists there and he wanted to know what the truth was. He had heard that we were in Trujillo, and had gotten a good report on what we were teaching and how we were living there. We had plenty of time. It is sometimes a great difficulty not to have the time to explain things, and when people are indoctrinated with Seventh Day Adventism, it's a little bit difficult. They have been taught the doctrine, their doctrine, and will keep to certain portions of God's word, while ignoring others. There may be some hope, but they cling to this narrow path about keeping the Sabbath day. It's a rather difficult thing to get them out of Exodus Chapter 20. That's where they stick. Once you can get them past that, there is more hope.

I saw at once that this dear man was open to listening. The

Adventists great ambition is to teach, if they're not teaching you, then often they won't listen. I have had them get up and leave, saying "you're teaching me now and that's not permitted." But this man listened very attentively, and we began at the first, in Genesis.

God rested on the Sabbath day, didn't He? Sure He did, but He never gave Adam and Eve the commandment to rest on the Sabbath day. He rested. He was the one that rested. Why? He was the one that was doing all the work. They had done nothing, so when His work was finished, He rested. But He didn't rest very long because sin came in. Sin came in and ruined the work and God had to start to work over again. As we are told in the gospels, the Lord Jesus Christ himself said, "My father worketh hitherto, and I work," when he was accused of not keeping the Sabbath.

Slowly we made our way through the Old Testament, and then we came to the first time when the Sabbath was mentioned. I drew his attention to whom God gave the order to keep the Sabbath day. It was to His own earthly chosen people that he had given that commandment. He did not give it to the Philistines or all other nations. And He gave it for a certain purpose; He gave it as a sign. It was a sign between Him and them, exclusively. It was for God's own earthly people alone. Then He told them how the Sabbath was to be kept. I explained all that to him.

I explained also how the Lord Jesus Christ, because of sin, came down to earth. He had to work and work hard to pay the price. He shed His precious blood before the work was finished. Then when the work was finished, poor sinners all over the world could put their faith and trust in Him and they would receive forgiveness of their sins. That was the principle thing that he wanted to know. I was able to explain it to him in such a way that he received Christ as his Savior.

Not only did he receive Christ as his Savior, but a wonderful work was started there. I was occupied all week preaching the gospel in the evenings and, during the daytime, I was in conversation with that dear man who invited me, as well as with others who showed interest. At the same time, of course, I visited every home, leaving the gospel with the dear people living there. Don Antonio and Don Pedro, the two young men who brought the message that their father wanted to speak to me, and a younger brother, Don Cuto, all accepted the Lord Jesus

Christ as their Savior. And as time went on, others were saved, too.

One notable young man was Don Claudio. Don Claudio was a very intelligent young man. He showed much interest right from the first, and he did not sit down and wait on others. He went to Mexico, and took a course in dentistry and came back home ready to extract teeth. That was one great need among those dear people. In fact, along most of the north coast of Honduras, there are very few doctors and very few dentists. So this young man received a diploma for pulling teeth and started in. In that way, he was able to earn his own living, and, at the same time, use his time to preach the gospel. God used him, and very soon he was going all over that area, extracting teeth and preaching the gospel. He kept studying and reading the Scriptures and he became a good teacher. He became one of the best. He had a family of 13 and that alone kept him extracting teeth.

Don Cuto, the youngest of these boys that had accepted the Lord, was taken in by a family in Trujillo and they taught him many, many things. He excelled in baking, baking bread, and developed quite a business. He became one of the chief men of the brethren in Trujillo. So you see, God, in a wonderful way, used that family for many things.

Now, at the same time, while distributing the gospels, I met another very interesting man. He was coming up to a 100 years of age. You don't find that so often down there. He told me many interesting things about his people. There was a tribe of Indians living on the south coast of America. In those days, the sailing boats passed by near where they lived so they made big canoes out of trees, very big canoes. They went out by the hundreds into the ocean, preying upon the sailing boats that went by, robbing them of all that they had.

On one occasion, so he told me, a big storm came up and they were unable to return to their own villages. The wind and storm took them on and on and on until they came to the British West Indies. There they landed on those islands. They killed off all the men and took the women as their wives. Very soon they multiplied.

At that time, England sent one boat per year to collect all the fruits and spices and everything else produced on those islands. As time went on, the British found something mysterious happening. They'd leave a governor to take care of a few of those islands, but when they came back in a year they'd find that the governor had died. He'd contracted a disease like malaria and wasn't there. That kept on for years until the British became more and more suspicious of what was happening. On one occasion, they left to go home as usual but returned after two weeks. They discovered that as soon as they had gotten out of sight, these people had taken the governor and killed him. The British, of course, got very angry with these people. They sent quite a number of gun boats out, put them all on the boats and brought them up to the three islands the British held at that time off the coast of Honduras (Roatan, Guanajoa and Utila). (Remember the name Utila. We will come across that place again later on.) They left them there on those vacant islands.

With time, they began to make boats again, canoes. The islands soon became too small for them and in that way they came across to the north coast of Honduras. Today, they can be found right from British Honduras along through a very small part of Guatemala and into Honduras. That is the reason the Carib Indians are there today, so this old man told me. They had multiplied along the coast because they were fishermen.

Speaking about fish, if you are in a Carib Indian village for any length of time, that's what you will eat; fish, fish and more fish. The men folk get up early in the morning, about 2:00, 2:30, and off they go to fish. They come back home again about 7:00, or maybe a little later, and have their fish with them. They like the small fish, about 6 to 9 inches. Don't ask me what it is. I can't tell you the name. As a rule, I found it very useful in traveling about to wait and see how the people eat, then I would follow suit, but I would advise you not to do that when it comes to the Carib Indians eating fish. After it's cooked, they get the head with one hand and the tail with the other and put it in their mouth like a harmonica. They keep pushing it and spit out the bones as they go along. They can do that at a great high speed, but I never attempted it. I'm sure I would have gotten into trouble by swallowing the bones.

They also have a bread called *casabe*. It's made out of the yucca plant. I have got a little of this casabe here in my hand. It is only 18 years of age, that's all. I don't know any bread like this. After they have it baked and all, they store it in barrels. They keep many barrels of it there so they always have food in the house. But you'd also better know how they eat this bread. It's good, but sprinkle it first with water and then eat it. If you don't, it will swell up in your stomach.

Their staples are fish and casabe. They have no coffee, however. You won't get coffee there and you won't get the kind of tea we're accustomed to, but they'll give you some lemon grass tea. They just go out and pick a little of that lemon grass that's growing all over and bring it in and brew it. Thank the Lord for this casabe, though. I've used it in many illustrations among the children. It's like no other bread. It's like the bread of life. It's always good. Although this particular piece of bread is 18 years of age, right now, well, if I was hungry enough, I would eat it and it would stop the hunger.

They also eat *tortuga* (turtle) eggs. The turtles come out of the ocean during the night and the Carib Indians go down to the beach and look for the tracks. They are like a tractor track. The tracks lead them to where they have laid their eggs, so they can pick up about 50 eggs or so at a time. Now, I don't advise eating them boiled, but, they are very nice when they're scrambled. Otherwise, they're rather difficult to get down and, if they do get down, they might upset your stomach as they did my wife's. That meant that she was rather sick for a little while until she vomited them up.

So there you have it. That's what you have to eat if you're down there among them. I think they have a very healthful and joyful life, those Carib Indians. I know no one that lives as carefree as they do, and I've spent many happy days in their villages.

# CHAPTER 22: A Trip into the Mosquito Jungle Four Months Later

## Notes on a trip to Carib Villages:

**6th August.** Left Trujillo 6:30 a.m. bound for Carib villages in the Iriona District. At noon arrived at the station Los Mangoes. Was fortunate enough to find a man and a boy who were willing to carry my baggage to Iriona for 35 cents, an hour's walk. On arrival there, I got fixed up at the *alcalde's* (mayor's) house. There I met a man looking for coconuts for the factory in La Ceiba. He, too, intended visiting the villages to see what prospects there were of securing coconuts. After a little rest and food we started off to the west of Iriona and a half hour's walk brought us to the Carib village La Punta. Here I left copies of the gospels in each house while my friend went about his business. We met at the other end of the village and later walked to another village called Iriona Vieja, another half hour's walk. I should have liked to spend more time in this village but, after distributing the gospels, it was necessary for us to get back to Iriona before dark.

**6 p.m.** Arrived in Iriona hungry and tired. The alcalde's wife had some black beans and rice and coffee and we made short work of all, including the ants which fortunately we could not see very well as it was nearly dark and lights of any description are not much used in these parts. Having my camp bed and mosquito net along with me, I had no trouble in finding a place to put my bed. The other man had neither but after some begging and borrowing and pleading, he was the happy possessor of a mosquito net for the night. After getting my bed fixed up with the net and when about ready to get in, I was advised that I had built my house on someone else's lot; I had to move over a few feet. In a short time, everyone had found a place (by this time there were quite a number of us), and I was soon asleep.

**Tuesday 7th.** Early in the morning I looked out through my net but could scarcely find a place on which to put my feet as the floor was all occupied by beds. Two prisoners were there; they were being brought down from the Mosquito District for stealing whiskey (native made). The man who accompanied me the day before joined with me in making arrangements with a Carib from La Punta to take us east of Iriona to the next village of Sangrelaya by canoe. When he arrived, we found the canoe too small for ourselves and baggage, so we sent on the baggage with him and decided to walk along the beach. An hour's walk brought us to Sangrelaya. After a short rest I went around the village with gospels and made arrangements to have a meeting that afternoon. The R.C. (Roman Catholic) priest had been there two weeks before and so everyone insisted on calling me "Padre". At noon we had some lunch. At 4 p.m. quite a number gathered to listen, and I had the privilege of explaining why I had come to their villages. They listened well and seemed pleased with the message. Some inquired where they could get a Bible.

While I was speaking, I noticed the R.C. church bells began to ring (this building or shack where I was speaking was just across the street) and soon a few women gathered. The priests only visit these villages once in four or five months to sprinkle the new babies and collect money. I walked out in the village about 20 minutes and distributed some more gospels in another place. In the evening we had fried eggs and plantain (fried bananas) for supper. Later we got our beds fixed up in a shack, and this time we had it all to ourselves. About 3 a.m. the other man woke me up as he thought a revolution was breaking out as there were several gun shots. This is very uncommon in a Carib village as these people are very peaceable. The shooting soon stopped and we lay down again. As daylight was breaking through the walls of the shack, which were made of palm leaves, I heard my friend jump out of bed and grab a hen, which with her 12 chickens had been troubling him, and throw her out the door.

**Wednesday 8th.** We are on the way to Tocomacho about three hours walk. We sent our things on by canoe. On our arrival at Tocomacho we found an old German living a short distance outside the village. He gave us a place to put our things in and to spend the night. In the afternoon I visited the village and left gospels in each home. Then at 5 p.m. had a meeting, which was well-attended. At least 35 men came while a number of women ventured as far as the door.

**Thursday 9th.** Had a good night's rest. It rained heavy all the morning. Walked down to San Pedro, another village a short distance away, and distributed gospels. Intended going on to Batalla in the afternoon but it rained. In the evening had a good meeting in San Pedro. At the end of the meeting I told any who had questions to speak out. One man asked why the priest charges three pesos to baptize children. This gave me an opportunity to explain a few more things contained in God's word. Before this meeting I spent some time teaching the children who had followed me about all day the names of the first man and woman and boys, etc.

**Friday 10th. 5:30 a.m.** All ready for the road again but rain is falling. After some trouble, we succeeded in finding boys for the baggage. They all kick about the weight of one grip, and this is because it contains 1,000 gospels and no doubt is heavy. At last the bartering is over and the price is fixed at 62 cents. One hour's walk brought us to Batalla, and as my companion was going right on to Papallaya, I decided to go, too, as a canoe was just starting off and then call at Batalla on my way back. We passed Palacio on the way; this village I will also visit on my return journey.

**11 a.m.** Had lunch at the house of a Ladino, then got into the canoe and started on our way again. We reached Papallaya about 1:30 p.m., and after a short rest I started off with gospels. One man told me he was the sexton of the R.C. Church but that he had a Bible hidden, because the priests tried to get it from him once. I asked him if he could get the people together to have a meeting, and he said he would soon do that. When I returned later he went out of the house and gave two or three calls and in a few minutes we had a good company listening to the gospel. I then hurried on further down to visit a few houses in the outskirts of the village. We got fixed up for the night in a small shack which we shared with a hen and her brood. Outside about half a dozen pigs bombarded us every now and again. My fellow traveler suggested that no doubt the pigs were accustomed to sleeping in the shack and resented our being there. My sense of smell made me think he was right, but I was soon asleep and forgot everything.

**Saturday 11th.** This morning I said goodbye to my fellow traveler. He went on to a big coconut farm further on and, being at the end of the Carib villages, I started on my return trip. From this point on the Sambo tribe begins.

**7:30 a.m.** Am in canoe on my way back to Palacio and Batalla. Reached Palacio, which is a small Ladino village. Here I distributed gospels and then went on. Arriving in Batalla, I left copies of the gospels in each house and about 3 p.m. had a well-attended meeting. On the way back to Tocomacho. Traveled half the distance by canoe and the rest by foot as there is no way by water from one laguna to the other. The cost from village to village is about 75 cents for the canoe and the man.

**6 p.m.** Reached Tocomacho tired so I put up my cot and was soon asleep.

**Sunday 12th.** It rained pretty heavily all morning. I visited the old German's son and his Ladina wife. I found her very much interested. This man, although ungodly, had been brought up to read the Bible and had many times pointed out to his wife the foolishness of trusting in images. Now that I confirmed what he had told her, she seemed to be satisfied and said she would like to have a Bible. Had another meeting at 5 p.m. and good attention was paid to the Word. At the end of the meeting, I heard one say to the other, "This man is speaking the truth and he takes all he says from God's book." They asked me to come back again soon and some of them asked for Bibles.

**Monday 13th. 5 a.m.** Am on my way to Sangrelaya by canoe. Reached there at 8 a.m. Spent the day visiting and resting. At 5 p.m. had a well attended meeting, although it would have been larger but many were away working. Here also a number said they would like to have Bibles.

**Tuesday 14th 7 a.m.** Am on my way in canoe to the station at Sangrelaya where I will catch the train for home. Arrived at the station at 9 a.m. Train arrived 11:45 and was in Trujillo at 6:30 p.m. During this trip I visited the German whom I stayed with on my way from the Mosquito District. I found that the other German who had gone there to get solitude had committed suicide. I presented the gospel to him on my last trip, but he did not seem to care to listen.

John Ruddock
Trujillo, Republica de Honduras
Central America
30th August 1934

# CHAPTER 23: The Children of John 3 and 16

*For God so loved the world, that he gave his only begotten son, that whosoever believeth in him should not perish, but have everlasting life.* John 3:16

The love of God so vast and free. The love of God it is for me. The very best that there can be. I found it so. I found it so. Thank the Lord, thousands more have found it so, too. John 3 and 16 has been used by the Lord in the conversion of many, many poor sinners. It's a very well-known verse that many children here learned. When I was working among the children, I found one child barely 2 1/2 years of age who could repeat John 3 and 16. I tried every place I went, but I couldn't find another child to beat that. God has used that verse mightily. He has also used it in very many strange ways. I've used an Irish version of it in my work to demonstrate the verse for children: A little Irish boy in the city of Dublin was found by a policeman lying in a doorway. This kindly hearted policeman woke up the little boy and asked him why he was there. Why was he not in his own home? He replied that he had no home. Well, the policeman said, "Look here, you go to a certain street, at a certain number, knock on the door and someone will come out. You just say, 'John 3:16', and he'll let you in." He did and in he went.

Now, before I tell you the Honduran version of John 3 and 16, I will first fill you in with some little history about the place where Simon, the Mosquito Indian boy lived. The Mosquito District, also known as the Mosquito Coast, was his home. It is a piece of land that lies between Honduras and Nicaragua. It was a very much neglected part of Honduras, and that's where the trouble lay. It was little different from the rest of the country.

142

The Sambo Indians lived there. They seemed to have more of an English flavor. In the rest of the country, it was a Spanish flavor. Lying between the Carib Indian villages and the Sambo villages, we once found an old cemetery. We excavated 6 or 8 inches down in the soil and there we came on some tombstones. The Right Honorable William Pitt was etched on one. He must have been some relation to the famous Pitt family in England. There was also the family of Hewitt buried there, too. There were quite a few of these tombstones, all under soil.

One of them drew my attention because it was that of a little child. There must have been an epidemic among the children in that time, because there were quite a few children's graves. The dates were in the 1700s. This child's stone said, "Mourn not for me, for I am blessed, and in Christ's arms I take my rest." It was a little girl. I'm not sure whether it was one of the Hewitt's or one of the Pitt's. That part of the country was famous for many things. That's where the great lost White City is rumored to be, somewhere in the Mosquito District. After returning from one trip to the Mosquito Coast, a Mr. Fox from the New York Times looked me up. He was down to investigate the lost White City. He did all in his power to get me to go, but I was looking for lost black sinners not white cities. I had not much interest in the lost White City, although I inquired a little about it when I was down that way. Some said they had seen it at a distance, but when they got others to go with them to find it again, they couldn't. To this day, it hasn't been found yet. The lost White City was never found, yet many black lost sinners were found, and I think that's better still.

Simon's people, the Sambos, live a very primitive life. They sleep on the mud floor of their little huts. Their bed is made of the bark of a tree. Their bed coverings are tree bark, too. In fact, I have seen some of the dear women folk use it as a skirt. The rest of the tree comes in very handy at times for them as well. They have enemies, and one of the chief enemies seems to be the evil spirits. They're troubled quite a lot by these evil spirits. If one took seriously sick, for example, they would put blame on the work of an evil spirit. They would call in the witch doctor who would direct a dozen to 18 boys to go out in the forest and cut down some sticks. They should be 6 feet high, or a little more, and about 1 or 2 inches thick. The boys would pound them into the ground very close together to make a kind of a circle. They'd leave just space large enough for two people. The sick person is put inside. The witch doctor goes in, too. Quite a

number of witnesses stand outside. Their duty is to watch for
the evil spirit going out of that little circle. The witch doctor en-
ters and performs his many activities. At last, out goes the evil
spirit. I would suggest that the evil spirit had been fixed up before, using glow worms or flies that produce a light. There are
plenty of light bugs down there. After he performs enough, he
throws a bowl full of these bugs through the opening, and the
crowd outside gives a cheer. The evil spirit is gone. Then the
witch doctor comes out as fast as he can. While several boys
close the opening so that the spirit will not find its way back in.
That poor patient then stays there for some time to make sure
that there will be no more trouble. They are very primitive people, as I said. They make their villages near a river where they
have water and fish. They also hunt animals, wild pigs or anything else they can find. There are lizards, too, of course.

The Sambos don't eat as we do. Perhaps they won't eat for
three or four days, but when they do eat, boy do they eat. They
eat everything there is. It was rather nice food at times when
you didn't know what it was. I always advised everybody who
set it before me, "Don't tell me what it is, and I'm all right." I
found that was the best way. My mother taught me that. Eat
what is set before you and ask no questions. I didn't ask any
questions. The iguana, or sometimes a snake steak, was very
good. You can see that an iguana isn't very palatable when it's
running about but on the table, it's very nice, very like chicken.
So they live on those things. Now then they are very different in
many other ways. But I think we have told you enough so that
we can go on now to the real part of the story, and tell you
about what God did with John 3 and 16.

One time I was told that a small gasoline power boat was to
call in at Trujillo and perhaps go down the coast the length of
the Mosquito District. I started to prepare for the trip. There is
no money used where we're going. So we'll pack our bags full
of ornaments of all description and plenty of aspirins, other
pills, and any malaria medication we can put our hands on. Of
course, the main cargo was the gospel of St. John, and that was
a rather heavy one. It was always heavy. Then Doña Nettie got
busy. She made some of her special bread, guaranteed to keep
good and fresh for over a month. She was a very good cook and
able to do some wonderful things. After waiting day after day
after day, which you inevitably have to do down there, at last
the boat came. We spent all that day and the next night traveling, and eventually got to Brus Lagoon in the Mosquito Coast.

There I spent the day among those dear Sambo Indians, leaving a gospel in each home. Then we found out that the people in the boat were going up the Patuca River. Of course, the gasoline boat was too big to go up the river, so we went up on a big canoe with an outboard motor. The canoe was full of salt and other provisions. These men were interested in alligator skins so up we went to a village, stopped there and found that they had quite a number of alligator skins ready. The skins were put on board and the salt was left for the alligator hunters. They'd skin the alligators and salt them to preserve them for the next trip. On and on we went up the Patuca River until darkness began to fall. When it did, we camped on the banks of the river. I tried to sleep, but I had to fight the mosquitoes practically all night. I'm not afraid of the mosquitoes, but I am afraid of malaria. They're very obliging; they'll give you malaria very easily. After you've had malaria a few times, the doctor will advise you that you've got to be very careful because the next Malaria may be black water fever. He can't guarantee your life once you get that. The next day we're off again and finally the hunters come to their journey's end. We found another big canoe and men willing to take us further up the river, another day's journey. As we went up the river, there were always small villages. I make arrangements to get off and visit the dear people.

Often, word had gone before us that the missionary was on his way. A missionary is often expected to perform all kinds of miracles. Each place we went, the halt, the lame, and the blind waited. Sometimes a few pills would help out. We'd leave more pills for when we were gone but above all we left the gospel of St. John. On and on we went until we came to near the end of the line, which happened to be a banana camp way far up the Patuca River. Some Germans had planted bananas in that no-man's land. They were trying to make a living. Money is of no use there so the Indians trade work for goods from the commissary, all kinds of goods and materials: shirts, pants, shoes, socks, whatever you like. When those men come in looking for work they don't ask how much they are going to earn. They look at a pair of shoes and ask how many days work must they perform to get those shoes. "Oh, those are good shoes. You have to work for 14 days to get that," the Germans would say. "All right," the Indians would reply, and the bargain was sealed. The name was put on the shoes and away they went to work. After 14 days they would come back and get their shoes.

I spent all my time possible reaching as many people as I

could. I was told that the boat was going back down river on a certain day, and if I wasn't there I might not get home for some considerable time. When the day came, of course, I had to wait a few days extra. It's always mañana down there. Those days soon went and I got on the boat and went to Brus Lagoon. There, I made arrangements to get home. Now there was no gasoline to power the boat so I looked for a land guide. This guide was supposed to take me to a certain lake where they'd find a little boat, *cayuco* they called it. From there, we'd cross the lake and wouldn't have so far to walk. We got to the lake, but there was no boat. "Where is the boat?" I asked. "Oh, I know where it is," my guide said. "Someone came along here and wanted to go to the other side. They took the boat and it is at the other side of the lake waiting for someone coming back, but no one has come back yet." "What will we do?" I asked. "Can you walk?" he said. "Sure, I can walk," I said, "but can you?" He laughed.

We started to walk. We walked and walked and walked and walked until we had to walk some more again. At last we got to a place where we could stay the night. The next morning, the contract was that he was to take me on to where the train stops, but the poor guide lost himself. There we were, in big tall grass, and you couldn't see a thing. He had lost his way somehow, and now we're in this tall grass wandering about. At last he said, "You'd better stay here. You'd be too tired, I'm sure. I'll go and look for the path." And away he went. I got a funny feeling after I had been there for about an hour. I was beginning to get hungry and tired. Finally he came back. I noticed, as he had left that he had his machete working. He explained that was how he marked his way to the path. Now all we had to do was walk for 15 minutes and there was the railroad. He went his way home, and I waited for the train. Of course, it was a banana train, where every banana is a guest and every passenger is a pest. I was able to flag the train down and, although I was a passenger and not a banana, they welcomed me on board. The train was late as ever, and I was rather late in getting home. I had to wake my good wife up out of a nice sleep. She did not take long to prepare a meal fit for a king, and my, how I enjoyed it. She could turn out some wonderful meals. That is a little background on the Mosquito District where that little Sambo Indian boy lived.

As I said, the little boy's name was Simon. One day he was running along a narrow path with high grass on each side of him when, suddenly, he stopped. He saw something that was very rare to see in that part of the world at that time. What was it? It was only a little piece of paper, but you don't often meet a little piece of paper there. No, paper is very scarce in the jungle. They used banana and other leaves instead of paper to wrap purchases. He lifted this piece of paper very carefully. There might be a scorpion underneath it or something. He finally got it up and what do you think was printed on it? It was John 3 and 16, that's what it was. One of those St. John gospels that I'd given out had evidently fallen into the hands of one who did not care for such a thing, and they had torn it up. You see, God often uses his enemies for His honor and for His glory. Little Simon lifted it up. Thank the Lord he was able to read a little, which many of those dear people cannot do. He looked at it and read: "For God so loved the world that He gave his only begotten Son, that whosoever believeth in him shall not perish, but have everlasting life." He did not understand it. He did not know very much about love in any way. And, as for God, well, who was He? However, he thought it was a wonderful thing. He began to repeat it until he could say it by memory. He called it his own.

As time went on, he grew to be a young man. He had heard of the big world that existed outside of the Mosquito District, and he often heard how things were wonderful there. He had wished that he could make a trip to the big world outside. Eventually he was able to do that. The only way he had to go was on foot so he started off and he walked and he walked and he walked and then he walked some more. It took him some considerable time to eventually walk to Trujillo. In Trujillo, like in many of the other towns in Honduras, there is a central park that is used much for socializing. Simon walked by the little gospel hall right in front of the park. It was a big room in the house that we had rented. As he walked by, what do you think he heard? "...for God so loved the world that He gave his only begotten Son." He stopped quickly. What's that? Where did I hear that before? And then he remembered how it was that he had found the paper as a little boy in the jungle with those words printed on it. Sad to say though, the meeting was over. I had been the only speaker there for many months and I generally closed the gospel meeting quoting John 3 and 16. The congregation went out the door and the meeting ended.

The next day, away Simon went to find the train to take him to a banana camp. He found one and he inquired for work. Of course they could give him work. Did he have a machete? No, he didn't have a machete. They gave him a machete on credit and he started to cut bananas. That night it was dark because there was no electricity, but he saw a light shining in the sky. It was the gasoline-powered Coleman lamp that the Christians used to enlighten gospel meetings. He saw the light, and then he heard some singing. He made for the direction of the light and the singing. When he got near the place, what do you think he heard? "...for God so loved the world, that He gave his only begotten Son." That was the third time he'd come into contact with that wonderful verse. This time, he didn't wait. He went to the meeting, he told me afterwards. When he got there, they were just finishing quoting John 3 and 16. He was invited in and he sat down. The dear brother explained something about John 3 and 16. He brought out man's need; he told them how each had sinned against God and how that sin was going to take them to a place of punishment in eternity. He was very faithful in bringing out some common sins down there. Simon listened, taking in every word. At the end of the meeting he stayed and someone came down and spoke to Simon. With tears in his eyes he asked them, "Please explain more." They did, and then he said, "Ahhh, yes. I understand it now. I know what it is now." God saved him there and then.

The first time I met Simon, he had organized a Sunday school. I hadn't visited that town for some time. When I got there, they told me about him. He was getting the children together and teaching them John 3 and 16. When I was introduced to him he told me his story. And he asked me a question: "Where could I get about one hundred John 3 and 16s?" I said, "I could get them to you very easily. What do you want them for?" "I want to go back and visit my people in the village, and take them the wondrous story that I have heard here." I got him the gospels and away he went. I'm sure that God used those messages, for today there are Christians there.

# CHAPTER 24: Reaping the Harvest

Back in the middle 1930s, the Holy Spirit began to work in a remarkable way on the north coast of Honduras and, more or less, that work has continued until this day. At that time, many notable characters got saved, and we'll tell you about some of them. We were living, my wife and I, in Trujillo in that time. We were all alone in the world. Allen Ferguson and his wife had returned to the U.S. Brother Hockings and his good wife had gone to England for a little rest. So it was necessary to make many trips from Trujillo to San Pedro Sula and back again for business and supplies.

On one of these trips, when I arrived in La Ceiba, Brother Zelaya wanted to know if I could wait over the next day to visit a dear lady who was in trouble. He said she was very anxious for us to go and have a conversation with her. I thought of Philip and although I was on my way home, I thought, like Philip, that I had better stay. So stay I did.

This dear lady, Doña Mariana, lived in a village not so very far from Ceiba. She seemed to be a rather brilliant lady, rather remarkable in many ways and a good woman, as far as goodness goes in this world. She took pride and interest in her people, especially newborn babies. She tried to keep track of each new baby when it was born and who its parents were, so that when the priest would come, she could guide him to these homes so that these children could be baptized, securing, she thought, their entrance into heaven.

On this occasion, when she had quite a list, she sent for the priest who lived quite a distance away. He sent back a message that he could not come. Why could he not come? Because the last time that he was there, they did not have enough money for him. That preyed upon this dear lady's mind. What is this? she thought. Why does God, if you can believe in God, make such laws as this? Before these children are one year of age, 50% will have died. What about them then? This thought continued to prey upon that dear woman's mind. She didn't know what to do. She began to doubt God. There is no God, she said. If there is a God, he'd be a God of love, he'd be considerate, he would know that these poor people do not have the $1.50 to pay for the baptism of each child. No, there can't be a God. There is no God. That was the conclusion Doña Mariana came to. She figured, if there was a God, he would not oppress the poor people. She became a temporary atheist.

She went on passing the days, trying to forget all about the poor children, trying to forget all about God. It was a mess that she could not understand. She went on like this for days, until one afternoon she sat in the front door of her little shack and she saw the sun setting in the west. Where is the sun going to? she thought. Where does it go after it leaves here? It's going to God. No. There is no such thing. There is no God. No. That can't be so. That's how she figured it out. Then she began to think of something that she had heard. She had heard of a certain class of people called *evangelistas* or gospelers. She had been told that they were a good people. She had heard that they were very considerate in all things. She had heard many good reports about them but, on the other hand, she had been advised by her church to beware of those kinds of people. They were only deceivers, you couldn't believe them, they were spreading false teachings, she was warned by the church. She was advised to keep away from them out of all other people.

She began to think more seriously that perhaps it could be that they have something and know something that we do not. So she began to inquire about these people. There were no evangelistas in her village, but she had heard that there were some living in La Ceiba. After getting permission from her husband, which is a very necessary thing down there, off she went to La Ceiba. She did not know where to go when she got there, but she began to inquire. She walked from house to house and knocked on doors. "Pardon me, could you tell me where the evangelistas are?" No, they couldn't tell her. She walked about all afternoon. She could not find anyone to give her the information she sought. She got up early the next morning and started off again, inquiring from door to door.

There was a seeking sinner. There was someone who was ready for the gospel and that's the first thing that the sinner needs - he needs to be ready. She was ready. She was seeking a savior. Oh, that she could only find Him. At last, she was told, "Yes, there is a man. He is an evangelista. He's a very good man, but he lives away in the other part of the city." She was given direction, and off she went, on foot, of course. Eventually, she got to Zelaya's home. She inquired, "Is there an evangelista here?" "Yes, by the grace of God, there is," Zelaya answered. "Come right in. Have a seat." "I'm very anxious to have a talk with you," she said. "I've heard a lot about you, but I'm afraid I don't have time now. I've only permission from my husband to stay until now." "Never mind," Zelaya told her. "Give me your direction, and we will go out and visit you."

Instead of continuing my journey home to Trujillo, I went along with Brother Zelaya to help this dear woman. Zelaya had time just to tell her not to trouble about the children, that God had taken care of them. It was older people, at the age of responsibility, who were in danger, and that worried her to think of her own condition. She had some important questions to ask. It was quite a joy to sit down with her and explain many things from the Scriptures. You remember she had come to the conclusion that there was no God because if there was a God he would be a God of love. According to her experience, there was not much love demonstrated by sending little children to perdition because their parents didn't have enough money to have them baptized. However, Brother Zelaya put her straight on that matter. The first thing to do was to see her own condition, then, after that, she may be able to see to the condition of others.

We brought John 3:16 before her. There we pointed out that God is a God of love. That He loved the poor sinner so much that He sent His only son; that the Lord Jesus Christ was born into the world by the Virgin Mary and the Holy Ghost; that He did not enter earth as any other man; that He grew up and, eventually, when the time came, carried out the work that God had sent Him for. He went to the cross and, there on the cross, He received the punishment for our sin, the punishment that every sinner should, without the gift of Christ's salvation, receive throughout eternity. Brother Zelaya was very straight and frank and plain in telling her that these idols, which she had been worshiping at the church, made out of wood, stone and precious metals, were only works of man's hands, and they could never save anyone. But the Lord Jesus Christ, who received the punishment that every man, every sinner, deserved, could save anyone who desired it from that eternal punishment. All that remained to be done was to put her faith, trust and confidence in the Lord Jesus Christ as her Savior. I left much of the talking to him, as he was well versed in all of those important things. He brought out to that dear lady, very effectively, what was needed for her soul's salvation. The work had been done. All she had to do was put her trust in it. It wasn't a question of doing. It wasn't a question of buying. It wasn't a question of money. He told her there were no lempiras (Honduran currency) in heaven; no dollars in heaven. That was an earthly thing and, when it came down to it, that was man's doings, not God's.

After some time of explaining, her face seemed to light up. "You don't mean to tell me that I've nothing to do?" she said. "No, absolutely nothing." "Well, I've been 'doing' all my life." "Yes," Zelaya said. "And, so had I, until that night I put my trust in the Lord Jesus Christ as my Savior and, sure enough, the light seemed to dawn." Before we knew it, she was preaching to us, telling us how God could save a sinner.

At last, I said, "Tell me, if you were to die tonight, where would you go?" "I would go to heaven," she said. "You're going to heaven? Aren't you a sinner? Haven't you sinned against God?" "Yes, I deserve to die, I deserve to be punished, but the Lord Jesus Christ received the punishment for me." And we all got down, and we thanked the Lord for saving her soul. Yes, Doña Mariana, after being deceived for so many years, came to the point of simplicity and received Christ as her Savior. When Doña Mariana received Christ as her Savior, she truly turned from idols to serve the living and true God. Indeed, she was quite active for the Lord. Brother Zelaya, not living so very far from her, was able to visit quite often. She had many questions. She was very eager to grow in knowledge of the Lord Jesus Christ, her Savior. Of course, she asked about baptism. So, Zelaya took the time to explain about baptism. Baptism was not for newborn babies, he said. There was no such thing found in the Scriptures, the Scriptures say that those who receive Christ as their savior are to be baptized. She was very eager to be baptized. When the opportunity came, she took that step. Baptism was a wonderful but trying step to take in those days, in those places. Often new Christians were excommunicated, driven from their homes and had to suffer in other ways. However, the Lord put Doña Mariana in a wonderful way, and she was able to lead her own sister to Christ. Some time passed and her husband passed away. He had been a very delicate man, and had been ill for many years. They had no children, so she, along with her sister, her sister's husband and her sister's children, moved from where they were living to Tela. We, too, were living in Tela at that time. She was a wonderful help to my wife in many ways.

One Sunday afternoon, Doña Mariana went out for a walk. As she was walking through Tela's streets, down near the beach, a man drew near. They looked at each other and she realized it was her brother who she had not seen for years. "Pancho!" she exclaimed. "Mariana!" he said. And then they were in each other's arms. It was a wonderful meeting. He hadn't known whether she was even alive. After a little conversation, she asked him what he was going to do at the moment. He had just come out for a walk, he said. He thought he'd come to Tela, as he heard there was work there. "What are you going to do this evening?" she said. "Not one thing. I have nothing to do." "Then you'll accompany me to the gospel meeting up in the chapel," she said. But go to the chapel, that was another thing. "You don't mean to sing?" he said. "You go there, do you?" "Yes," she said. She did, and that kind of frightened the poor man because that's where the devil was. Yes, that was his headquarters, so he had been told.

He told me afterward that on one occasion he had the opportunity of passing through a village where there was a little chapel. Upon hearing that the devil made his headquarters there, he was very, very afraid to pass by that way. He got a little courage up and went past the door and he couldn't see the devil. He wanted to see him, so he walked by again, a little slower this time, but he still couldn't find him, so he left it alone. They told him afterward, "Yes, but you didn't go inside. He's up behind what they call the platform. That's where he is. Hiding in there." He said that he was very much afraid to go with Doña Mariana, but he did, he did. What he heard that night was something that he'd never heard before. He not only heard, but he took it in. And while he was not singing that night, when he came back again, he took his place as a sinner and received Christ as his Savior. So it was that Don Pancho, like his sister, became a new creature in Christ Jesus. Simply by taking his place as a sinner and receiving Christ as his savior.

Don Pancho was a woodsman. He'd go up into the mountains and cut down trees. Then by hand, he'd cut them up into boards so they could be used for house building, furniture, or anything else that required boards. It happened to be that I needed some wood. I was about to build. We gave Don Pancho, along with two other brethren, Don Blas and Don Salvador, the contract to cut the wood. They went up into the mountains, after securing permission and paying the tax. They went up there, cut it by hand and brought it down. We paid them five cents a foot for good cedar wood. They spent the week up there, but came down on Saturdays.

At that time, I was making trips down the coast on the first part of the week so that I was always back on Saturday. Saturday night was the night for the Christian's meeting where I opened up the word and taught. The principle teaching in those days was baptism and the Lord's supper, gathering together the first day of the week in His Name alone. I also taught a little about the Lord's coming. Those three subjects were all that were necessary for the moment for those dear new Christians to learn quite a lot. Indeed, many came down from the mountains and other nearby assemblies to be at that meeting on Saturday night. My wife had a meeting for children and young people on Saturday evening. All wanted to learn English, so that was a good opportunity to get them into the chapel. I was there in time to give them a little Scripture lesson and then we invited them to stay on for the meeting afterward. Those were wonderful days. The Lord came in and taught those dear Christians many things that they were able afterward to go back to their own assemblies and teach others. That was the idea.

Don Pancho was very much interested in those subjects. They were subjects that he had never heard in the church that he had been connected with. What he learned was very different, when he saw it in the Bible, from what he had been used to. Pretty soon he was able to help in teaching the gospel, which he did on Sunday nights. In fact, it got to be that I was not necessary on Saturday and Sunday nights because we had so many others to preach the gospel. Souls were saved who had come in to listen to the message. All those dear Christians living on the coast came from a distance. Their own homes were in the jungle villages and mountain tops. Many of them were anxious to go back to their own village with the message.

So, in time, Don Pancho, Doña Mariana, their sister, and a cousin who was saved, along with the children, started back to their own village to tell the good news to their families. It was a long, dusty, tiresome journey, mostly on foot – up the rough mountainside, down the path into the valley and up another mountain again. At last their little village came into view. Upon arrival, of course, there was great joy and rejoicing because they all belonged to that little village. Some of them had been away for some time and they got a royal welcome. However, as two or three days passed, Don Pancho and Doña Mariana began to tell the good people of that village their experiences in coming to the knowledge of the truth. It did not go down very well with some of the villagers but as the Scriptures say, "The truth will make you free" and some believe and some believe not. Quite a number believed, though some didn't.

Doña Mariana, her sister and the children returned to Tela, but Don Pancho remained there and, of course, he was not idle. He had a new work to do now – as well as cut wood – and he did it. He began to preach the gospel to the people around him. Pretty soon more were saved, baptized and soon another little assembly was formed.

Years later, when we were leaving Honduras to retire in the States, the dear Christians in Tela had advised all the assemblies of our imminent departure and set a day to say good-bye to us. Before that day came, we saw an old man with a stick trying to make his way up the 50 steps to our house in Tela. Who could it be, bent over, trying to make it up the stairs? It was Don Pancho. "Ohhh, Don Juan," he cried, "Is it true? Is it true?" "Is what true?" I asked. "You're going away to leave us? Tell me you're not." "Oh," I said, "it's true. This old body won't stand it any longer. I've got to go. I'm no more use here." "Well, Don Juan," he said. "Thank you, thank you, thank you for ever coming to Honduras. Thank you for the message you brought us." We parted from each other, in each other's arms. The tears running down our faces. Can I ever forget that?

Doña Mariana was not idle, either. Upon returning from her village back to Tela, she and her sister made a living by baking and selling bread. However, Doña Mariana continued to be very active in the spiritual side of things. She was a great help to my wife in many, many ways. She was wonderful in the Sunday school and also in the daily vacation Bible school. She was a wonderful help in the sisters' missionary meetings held in many parts of the north coast. She became a favorite among the sisters in many places. However, soon she remarried to one of the national social workers. She went with him to the village of San Juan Pueblo, which is not so very far from Tela. There, she began to work among the children, and very soon there was a little gospel meeting in their home. As time went on, God saved some souls and a little assembly was formed. She had a great heart for those who had received Christ as their Savior and tried to keep track of where they lived.

As I mentioned before, Don Salvador was the one, along with Don Pancho and another brother, who had cut the wood for our home. There was not much work, and he and his wife and children had gone to live in the mountainside. There they could get a little living out of sowing their own corn and beans, but we hadn't heard from him for a long, long time. My wife was very anxious about him. Where could he be, what was he doing, and what condition was he in? It preyed upon her mind so much that she and Doña Mariana left to go and look for him. They were told it was a long way on a difficult, dangerous road, but nothing like that would stop them. They started off very early one morning. Up the mountain they went. Those paths, at times, are a little difficult to keep on. As you travel along, you must watch for smoke, a rooster crowing or a dog barking. They all indicate some sign of civilization. They found the place at last. He was there, but not in very good circumstances. He became cold in heart because he did not have fellowship with other believers. However, he was wonderfully pleased to see them. "Why? Why? Why did you come up here? Why did you come all this way?" he asked my wife. "We came up here to look for you. To see how you were. And your family," she responded. "You came to see me?" "Yes, we came to see you." After some little time in conversation, they convinced him that he'd better come down to San Juan Pueblo, which he did. There, at that time, they were about to build a little gospel hall so he spent time cutting the wood for the building. He went on to become quite a help in the work there because he had not been forgotten by the fellow believers. Doña Mariana kept busy in the Lord's work for some considerable time.

# CHAPTER 25: A Mosquito Attack

## Notes on a trip to Santa Rita:

**Friday 2 a.m.** Up and off to Santa Rita on the Mixto train. I am seated on the train and behind me are two women and a man. They are telling each other about their experiences in a machete fight, in which so far as I can gather one man was killed. There are very few passengers here in first class, but there are plenty of mosquitoes. I do not know where they all are going. How they can bite. But I have fooled them today as I have on my long-legged boots and they find the leather tougher than my skin, and so my ankles are safe.

"Hello." The man in front of me has declared war on the mosquitoes. He has just stuck his legs and feet into a sugar sack, has wrapped his head in a towel and is using another one as a mosquito killing weapon, and is his arm going? He seems to be gaining, for the mosquitoes are retreating, and it is not an orderly retreat, either, or according to plan, I should say. But here they come this way, several divisions of them, and I mean divisions, too. The train has just stopped at Kilometro 10 and several more divisions have joined their companions as reinforcements. Now it is war in earnest. Everyone is stamping their feet and swatting for all they are worth. And this is first class with all the windows and doors shut. When the door opened to let the passengers out, these fresh divisions forced their way in. What must it be in second class where there are neither windows nor doors shut. A child is crying sorely, and no wonder; it looks as if it would be impossible to walk up the aisle of the second class car as one can see nothing but towels, bags, handkerchiefs, etc., fly-

157

ing all directions. But I must stop looking and take care of myself. Now it is everyone for themselves. "Whack!" That's another
one less. They won't give ground an inch.

I wonder if the people at home ever think of how much the
soldiers suffer from these little insects in the tropics. I hope they
have plenty of quinine, atebrin, etc. (malaria medicine). We have
very little here. The train has just stopped at another station.
"Open the door and let the mosquitoes out," someone shouts.
"A good idea," says another. "Perhaps this is where they get
off." The doors were flung open, but instead of the ones inside
retreating, they got fresh reinforcements. "I have never seen the
like of this in my life," said the man behind me. His hands and
arms and legs were flying and looked all tangled up. Mama
(Nettie) would have said he was doing a "Highland Fling." It
was surely some kind of fling, and I imagine he needed a mas-
sage the next day, for I am sure his poor old muscles were
*asustado* (frightened). When he stopped his jig, I turned to look
at him. What a sight! His shirt was covered with blood. This, of
course, made me look at my own. I soon forgot his in looking at
my own. I thought perhaps I had cut my hand or something as
my shirt and hand were both bloody from the slain mosquitoes.
I must admit I had a sort of satisfaction in knowing that I had
done away with a number of the rascals. It was terrible, about as
bad as the night I slept on the banks of the Patuca River in the
Mosquito District when they came in thousands and in such
force that the mosquito net gave way and they chased me for
my life down into the river. It is getting worse every minute.
Now I have my raincoat out and am wrapping it round my head
and shoulders and am trying to keep my hands covered. This
had helped some, and I shall try to keep under cover for some
time now.

I finally have had to get out of my shell hole as I was nearly
suffocated and was afraid I would end up in a puddle of sweat.
But, alas, a fresh division is waiting on me and I am into the
thick of the fight again. The sun is rising and I hope it will help
disperse the enemy. I just see my old and faithful friend the bee
buzzing around. I did not recognize him at first and made a
swat at him as I was in the mood to swat at anything with
wings. I soon saw my mistake, however, and let him alone.
Pretty soon he took over, flying around and around, at times
dangerously near my nose or ear, but getting rid of the pests. I
wonder if the soldiers in the Solomons, etc., know how to let the
wild bees chase the mosquitoes for them.

**11 a.m.** The mosquitoes are practically gone, for which I thank the Lord. I know they will be back at night, but it is surely good to get a respite.

Aha, what's the matter? There is something wrong in the second class coach. It isn't much after all. A woman forgot to get off at the station, and now I see the empty gasoline cans, and other varied bundles go flying out of the window. "Oh, there goes the woman herself." She is making a dive to get off before the train gathers too much speed. And, like a woman, she got off the wrong way and certainly did not land on her feet, according to all the laundry I see. Everyone is enjoying the joke and cheering her. Poor woman, she surely did not get off in a dignified way. Now we are at the station of Uraca. I hear something outside. Two or three women are having a free-for-all. One evidently has been down on the ground already as her dress is all dirt and dust. One is trying to get on the train and the others are trying to get her off. The train is moving, and there is going to be a spill. Aha, there comes a man with a machete and he looks as if he will fix the three of them. Fix them he did. He pushed one onto the train and pushed the other two away from it, and then walked on as unconcerned as he could be.

Now we have 10 soldiers aboard with their rifles. They are in the second-class coach. One of them has just come down and he is ready to visit with us all. He is *alegre* (happy with drink) and looks as if he is going to be more alegre.

Now he has gone and is marching up and down the aisle of the second-class car as if on guard, but without his rifle. He is making good use of his tongue, however. Oh my, now there is a fight. He is going to fight another man; they have their fists up and are just ready to knock each other's noses off. The train has stopped, and it has knocked him off his feet and onto the broad of his back on the top of the other soldiers. The other man is on the broad of his back on top of some women, and are they yelling. It sounds like bedlam getting loose, and they are giving him some very ungentle shoves and pushes. Now the train is off again, and they are trying to find their balance. Now he has gone completely alegre. He has just taken his hat off and come bang down with the hat on the head of one of the soldiers. Now he has thrown it on the floor and is trampling on it like a Scotch woman washing her blankets; now he has picked it up and thrown it at someone else. Again he has his hat and is marching down towards us in the first-class coach. Everyone is expecting to get a swat of his hat, but no, he is marching straight on. My, if he hasn't walked right off the train and turned a somersault in doing so. Everyone thinks he is killed, but no, he is still marching right on without even looking back at us. I heard when I was a little boy that drunks have a special care, and I am inclined to believe it after seeing that stunt. Well, here we are at Santa Rita at 3 p.m. It has been a long ride, but no one can say that it has been lacking in amusement.

John Ruddock
Trujillo, Republica de Honduras
Central America

# CHAPTER 26: Laughter from the Valley

One day a brother named Don Pedro, who visited this out-of-the-way place called Trujillo, came to us praising the Lord for what he called miracles. He told us that he had visited his family's home situated in the heart of a mountainous district, with no near neighbors. Up to the time that the young man returned, the family had never heard the gospel. He said that, at first, some of the family scoffed and made fun of the Scriptures, especially one man who was huge in size and had a voice that sounded like a roar. But one night, in his rough way, he listened. The next day he went to his brother and said, "Give me that book. I want to know more about this nonsense."

The book was willingly handed to him and he went off into the mountains with it. He did this for three successive days. At the end of the third day, a voice was suddenly heard down in the valley, laughing. All recognized the voice and wondered what had happened. They soon found out, for he came up to the house waving the book, laughing with joy, and saying, "Now I see it. Now I see it." He clapped his brother Pedro on the back so hard that he said he was winded for a moment. And then, with tears, his brother said, "I see it now. Jesus died for me. Jesus died for me, and I accept Him as my Savior."

I wish I could transfer to paper the look on our brother's face as he told us this story. His eyes shone, as he shook his head he kept saying, "It is a miracle. Praise the Lord."

In this part of the country where these conversions took place, there is no pine wood for torches and, owing to war restrictions at the time, kerosene was very scarce. That meant that they had

little or no light at night, but that did not deter them from reading the Scriptures. Don Pedro told us that they gathered kindling, and two of the women folks kept a fire of kindling going
while one of the men read the Scriptures, and the others joined
in singing hymns. Then they got up very early in the morning
and again read the Scriptures and sang a hymn before starting
off to work on their land.

In a letter to assemblies in the States about Don Pedro at that
time I wrote: "One's heart burns as he listens to the story of
those children of God in their first love. May the Lord keep their
hearts ever on fire for Him. When I say they sing, don't think
that the hymns are sung as we do, but I do know that they certainly make a joyful noise unto the Lord."

We trust the Lord's people will picture in their minds this little
group of Christians in their little palm-thatched, dirt-floored huts
in the heart of the mountain, far from all the comforts of civilization. They gather around a fire of kindling for light, while a
brother points with his finger to each word as he goes along, la-
boriously and stumblingly reading the Scriptures that speak so
wonderfully of Him who was wounded for their transgressions
and bruised for their iniquities. And their hearts fill with a holy
joy. As the brother who told us about it said, it seems that the
very house is smiling in the midst of the mountains.

Once again we praise the Lord for answered prayer, and again
we ask our hearts if we shall again doubt. We have written this
letter so that God's people may rejoice with us in seeing their
prayers answered and with us shall praise the Lord for all His
faithfulness. We do thank our God for the many fellow workers
at home who so effectually labor with us in the gospel. May the
Lord bless each one and give joy in service for Him.

With warm Christian greetings, dear friends, and our thanks
for all your faithfulness.

Yours through grace,

John Ruddock
Trujillo, Republica de Honduras
Central America

# CHAPTER 27: Sinforosa Rojas, A Wicked Man

Sinforosa Rojas. What a man. What a wicked, cruel man. Sinforosa Rojas. He was the terror of the country. He carried two revolvers, one on each hip. He could use them both at the same time, pointed in different directions, and down would come his victims. Yes, everyone was afraid of him, even the authorities wouldn't face him. He was, indeed, a terrible man. But I'm thankful now to be able to say, "Sinforosa Rojas, oh, what a saint." What made the change in that dear man? Well, in the middle and late 1930s, when God began to work in a marvelous way in the north coast of Honduras, it was conference time in Santa Rita. In those days, there were not many Christians to attend because they were very, very few in number. Today, it is different, very much different. But when we first began the yearly conferences, the few Christians in that vicinity would get together and have a wonderful time. Friday, Saturday and Sunday in the mornings and again in the afternoon were sessions for teaching the Christians. But at night, it was the gospel, the good old story of Jesus and His love. It was during those evening half-hours that many miracles were wrought.

There we were that Saturday night. It was hot, very hot, and the Coleman gas lamp didn't make it any cooler. The bugs and flies attracted by the light didn't give much encouragement to the speaker. I was interrupted many times, having to spit out the bugs that got into my mouth. However, the audience was attentive. The Holy Spirit was working and souls were being saved. It was not an unusual thing during that time to see someone stand up and hear them say, "Yes, I receive Christ as my Savior." The gospel meeting was proceeding, and then an old familiar noise was heard, the revolver shots, way in the distance. Then they got nearer and nearer, until you could smell the powder, but God was still working. And then there appeared in the door a man. That man came walking up the aisle. When he got a quarter of the way up to me, he got down on his knees. He lifted up his hands and shut his eyes in prayer, but what was he praying? He told me afterwards, "Don Juan, I was praying that you would not panic. That you'd keep going on with what you had to tell." Yes, that's what he was doing. He was seeking the face of God in prayer, praying that there might be no disturbance, praying that the Holy Spirit would use the message in the hearts of those who were listening. No doubt his prayer was answered, for I found a new power and more courage to continue the message. What led this once evil man to become a dear saint of God? For the answer, we'll have to go back one year.

At the same conference the year before, he had a group of men who had an inclination to disturb the conference. On one occasion, when they were attempting to disrupt a meeting with revolver shots, something happened. He heard the message coming loud and clear through the air. Thank the Lord I had a very loud voice. "Be not deceived. God is not mocked. Whatsoever a man soweth that shall he also reap." That's what he heard. The word of God went home through his ear and down into his conscience. I went on to say, "Yes, friends, this is a time of sowing down here on earth, but remember the time for reaping is coming. What you sow now, you shall reap hereafter." That man remembered what he had been sowing. His life came back to him as he heard God's word. There he was. There were his men, but their outbursts were silenced. Those revolvers were quiet, but friends, the word of God sounded forth. The big guns of God's word were louder and more effective than man's invention, the revolver. And that dear man stood there listening. He was convicted of sin.

The Holy Spirit was working in his heart, but he left our company and went to his own home in Las Arojas, a short distance away from Santa Rita. He went to his bed, but he was disturbed. He couldn't sleep. He got up in the morning, still disturbed. What was he sowing? Yes, that is what haunted him. His many sins came up before him and he was more and more disturbed. He thought of his past life. He thought of how he had lived. He remembered many of the awful deeds that he had been occupied in, and he spent one week in distress. At last he thought he would look up some of these evangelistas, these people that he persecuted and despised. He sent a message to the principal brethren in Santa Rita. He invited them to come to his home. Now, when those dear Christian men received that message, they did not know what to do. Sinforosa Rojas wanting us to visit him in his home? They thought there must be something evil in this. They were afraid to go, and well might they be for they knew the sinister reputation of this man in years gone by. After much prayer, they went to other brethren and told them about the invitation. They prayed much about it. They sought God's face about it, and at last they said, "Yes. Yes. Perhaps God would have us go. He's enlightened us, so now we will go."

Preparations were made, and they went at the hour appointed by Sinforosa Rojas. As they went, one by one up the narrow jungle path, they were silent, not just because they were walking apart from one another, but because they were preoccupied with not knowing what to expect. However, they had prayed much, and consulted one another, and believed the Lord would have them to go. They got near the place and the door was open, as doors are nearly always open down in the tropics. Then they saw something that made their hearts jump. They saw a white table cloth on the table. That meant peace, and as they got nearer to the door, they saw that the table was well filled with nice things to eat, so they took heart. Sinforosa saw them coming and he came out to meet them. "Welcome," he said. "Welcome. Come right in." Then he told them why he had called them. He had had no peace of mind since that night when he had listened to the message during the conference, and the words were sticking in his heart. He couldn't get them out. "Be not deceived. God is not mocked. Whatsoever a man soweth, that shall he also reap." "I can't get peace," he said. "I know what my life has been before God, and before man. All the wickedness in my life has come before me in these past few days. And now I'm afraid. I'm afraid of the reaping time. I am convinced it is in the future and I've got to meet it. I've called you here today to tell me what I must do."

They lovingly told him, "It's true. You have been sowing. But you have been sowing something that could bring you a harvest of evil and torment for all eternity." They went on to explain that he was guilty before God. He said, "Yes, I know it." They went on to tell him that God is a God of love, that He had given

His Son, the Lord Jesus Christ, to die on the cross of Calvary for him, for his sins, for his life, for what he had been sowing in the past. They exhorted that dear man to put his trust in the finished work of the Lord Jesus Christ. They explained to him how the Lord Jesus Christ went to the cross and in those dark hours received the punishment for his sin, the punishment Sinforosa deserved for all eternity. They spent some little time with him, talking about these things. Then they told him, "Look, all you have to do is put your trust, your faith, your confidence in the Lord Jesus Christ as your Savior. Trust in what he has done for you." And they had the joy of seeing that dear man pass from death to life, from darkness to light, from living a life of wickedness to a life well pleasing in the sight of God.

Sinforosa Rojas was a wonderful testimony to the gospel and a power for the gospel ever after. He was a blessing to the work. He led many sinners to the Lord Jesus Christ and then God took him home before he was a very old age. Why? That so many times we can't understand, but perhaps his life work was over. Nothing more could he do for the Lord and, before the enemy could trip him up, which sometimes he does in such a case, God took him home to be with Himself. Some of us look forward to that day when we'll see him up there in glory.

# CHAPTER 28: A Two-Edged Machete

Don Eusebio Melgar was the man with the two-edged machete or, as we know it, the two-edged sword of the word of God. Don Eusebio was unlike many of those who we had to deal with down there. Don Eusebio had been a military man who had made many travels about in his revolutionary exploits. Somehow, he had the opportunity to hear the gospel, and when the word of God and the work of Christ were brought before him, he received Christ as his Savior before I knew him. Like many others, when there wasn't much doing in revolutions, he found work with the United Fruit Company. He was captain on one of the farms. He was in charge of quite a number of men. He saw to it that they got work started at the proper time in the morning – or at least near the proper time. One day he came to Trujillo where we were living. He inquired where we lived, came to the door and introduced himself. He wanted to have a conversation with us. That dear man was very anxious to know more of the Scriptures. He asked a lot of questions, questions about what the life of a man ought to be after he'd received Christ as Savior. Baptism was brought up as one of the chief things and, of course, we explained much more from the word. Eventually, he said, "Look here. You are just the people I am looking for." He told me where he was living and invited me to go to visit him, which I did. He began to grow in grace and in the knowledge of the Lord Jesus Christ. We found him to be a very able and useful brother. He was rather intelligent, and he gave a good help to the work in many ways. I'll mention one way.

We were having a daily vacation Bible school in Santa Rita. We had up to 100 children attend at a time. We'd have a wonderful time all week long before going on to another place; however, the local priest didn't think we should be there. He tried to make trouble, but Don Eusebio, being a military man, was well-posted in the laws of the land. So when the priest came to make trouble, Don Eusebio was the one who went out and spoke to him. He tried to get him to understand that we were living in a land of liberty, and the government of Honduras permitted us to come in to spread the gospel. That's what we were doing. When it came to the last night of the Bible school, the children were there, the parents had been invited and the priest came along, too. He stood at the door, and he caught each child coming and turned the boy or girl around and sent them home. Don Eusebio went out to the priest. "What are you doing? You know, you'd better be careful. You're breaking the law here." The priest then immediately went to the authorities. He went to the mayor of the town and the chief of police, and he brought them down with a number of policeman. He demanded them to send the children home. Don Eusebio stepped out and he said, "Look here, you'd better be careful you don't break the law of the land. Those inside here are walking according to the laws of Honduras, so be very careful." And then he read them the law.

The authorities stood outside and listened to Don Eusebio's message. At last, they told the priest, "Look here, man. You'd better go home. You'd better leave these people alone. Here they are doing a wonderful work. They're helping these children out. They're teaching them things that they ought to know, and they are taking an interest in the village here. We would advise you to go home and let them carry on with their work. They are not disturbing anyone. They are not interfering in any way with the people, nor are they breaking any laws of the land. You'd better forget about it and go home." There we saw the Lord frustrate the enemy who tried to make a disturbance and prohibit the spread of the good news of salvation. We had a wonderful time there, not only with the children but with their parents, too. We had the joy of seeing a wonderful work commence in that place.

Banana camps are made up of say 10 wooden houses joined together. This is called a *barracon*. There are about 10 to 30 barracones in each camp, according to the number of people employed. The barracones are set on posts 9 feet high. This leaves a big, open, unused space underneath, and it was very suitable for having gospel meetings. There was never any trouble looking for a place to meet, and the size of the camp dictated the size of the congregation you could get, from 50 people up to 200 people. Don Eusebio was very active in this kind of work. He was out every night preaching the gospel in one camp or another. God was using him and souls were being saved. There was much interest shown all around but, of course, there are always some who are against the spread of the good news. They would rather have a life of wickedness, of drinking, card playing, dancing or killing one another.

On this occasion, a friend of Don Eusebio's was passing by a certain house, and he heard the man of the house say something about Don Eusebio. He also saw him sharpening his machete. With files, they can sharpen those machetes to a very fine edge, like a razor blade. Every time his file came down on the machete he would sing, "If Don Eusebio preaches tonight..." And then he would sing what he was going to do. This friend of Don Eusebio thought that he had better tell him what this man, Don Alejandro, was saying about him. "Well," Don Eusebio said, "what he does not know is I've got a two-edged machete." When he was going back home in the evening, Don Eusebio's friend told Don Alejandro, "When I was passing here this morning, you were sharpening your machete, and you were saying what you were going to do if Don Eusebio would preach, but do you know that Don Eusebio has a two-edged machete?" "A two-edged machete?" He had never heard of such a thing. He had never seen such a thing. And that made him just a little bit afraid, but he was a man and he was going to face the two-edged machete, and away he went.

In this particular camp, where the meeting was to be this night, there was a piece of uncultivated ground. On this ground was growing some wild grass. That grass can grow up to 10 and 12 feet high. Don Alejandro got to that little patch of grass, and he hid in there. It was a good place to hide, and he knew that Don Eusebio had to pass by that way. He knew that if he were going to do anything, it would have to be in that place where he wouldn't be seen. As Don Eusebio was passing, he tried to bring down the machete. Now maybe some wouldn't believe this, but he told us afterward that that machete would not come down; his arm would not move; he stood there like a statue; and Don Eusebio passed by unhurt.

Then another rather strange thing happened. Don Alejandro found out that after he finally had the machete lowered, his feet seemed glued to the ground and he couldn't move; that was his testimony afterward. Don Eusebio started in with the two-edged sword (the word of God), and down he came with that sword, blow after blow after blow after blow. Every time it came down, those words went down into poor Don Alejandro's heart, and there he was, glued to the ground. He had to listen and he did listen. Don Eusebio didn't spare the blows. He spoke very plainly. He told of the wicked lives that they lived. He shouted, and he didn't know, of course, that Don Alejandro was even there. He said, "Hey, you over there. Didn't you have murder in your heart?" And that went down into Don Alejandro's heart in such a way that he was convicted of sin. After he got his feet loosened from the ground, he made his way home.

He spent a very, very uneasy night. He couldn't sleep. He was thinking of his sins. He was thinking of the message he had heard. He was thinking of the great evil that he was about to do, and still intended to do: take Don Eusebio's life. He had no peace. He had to get up early. He thought he had better go to the house of Don Eusebio. He thought he had better speak to him. He went. Don Eusebio wasn't up yet. He knocked at the door. Don Eusebio came out and said, "Come in." And the poor man said, "I couldn't sleep last night after what I heard you say. I've come here this morning to apologize, to ask your pardon, to tell you what was in my heart, what I intended to do. What can I do now?" Don Eusebio lovingly sat down beside him. He explained to him plainly the love of God and how He sent His Son as a sacrifice for our sins and the work of the cross of Calvary. The result was that the poor man took his place as a sinner that very morning and received Christ as Savior.

It was a wonderful thing to sit, as I had, in those meetings, remembering the Lord Jesus Christ and the finished work of the cross of Calvary. There was Don Eusebio and other Christians all united in love, remembering the one who had remembered them many years before when he took their guilty place on the cross of Calvary. Don Eusebio would come many Saturday afternoons and spend time with us. He also often spent the following day until the evening. He was very, very much interested in the Scriptures. We had the joy of teaching that dear man many things from God's own word. He was very faithful to the Lord.

That is what the grace of God can do, and that is what has been happening down in Honduras for many, many years.

On another occasion, when Don Eusebio came to visit us, he was very much downhearted. He was very much agitated and, indeed, he told us that he was in trouble. He explained the situation. Before God saved him, he belonged to the party currently out of power. He belonged to the Red party, and the Blues were in power at the moment. The big general who lived near where we were in Trujillo sent for him. When he sent for anyone, that meant he was in trouble. It meant that he was in danger, too, at times, so, Don Eusebio asked us to pray. We prayed earnestly that the Lord would come in and give him the needed help at this time. He was to appear in the general's office at a specified hour. After a time of prayer, away he went to keep his appointment with the general. The general was a very hard man in many ways, but at the same time he was a just man. The general questioned Eusebio for some time; Don Eusebio was very truthful. He answered him, "Yes, I belonged to the other party. I did at that time, but I do not belong to that party now. In fact, I don't belong to any party now." Don Eusebio explained why: "Because now I am under the influence and in the army of the Lord Jesus Christ." He told this dear general that he'd heard the wondrous story of the love of God, and about the work of Christ and the cross of Calvary. He told him how he had put his faith and trust in Him, and how he now was serving Him in truth and his life was changed. The general listened to him for some little time. Indeed, he knew what Don Eusebio's life was before, and now it seemed to be changed. Now Don Eusebio was not given to any disturbance; he was not stirring up the people to have another revolution; he was trying to help the country in another way; and, of course, when the general found out that he was working in connection with us, that settled it. He knew our testimony in the town, and he had agreed with many of our preachings and teachings. He told Don Eusebio not to fear. He would give him no trouble, as long as he didn't interfere politically in any way. Don Eusebio returned to the house overjoyed at what the general had told him, and he went back home again rejoicing in the Lord, more determined than ever to live for God and forget many of the other things that he had been occupied with in days gone by. Don Eusebio, the man with the two-edged sword, was quite a help in the work, and did many wonderful things to help the people out at the same time.

# CHAPTER 29: The Unwilling Bishop

During the lifetime of each one of us, there are a few days which are special in some way. On those days we may experience doubt, fear, confusion and utter helplessness. Such was the day when I was ordained bishop of the departments of Colon and the Mosquito District of Honduras. Just before leaving Trujillo to attend a conference in Santa Rita, we heard that a few "witch doctors" were brought in, roped up and put in prison. Not having much interest in witch doctors, we left for the conference forgetting all about this incident.

After the conference, when we arrived back home, the general in charge of that section of the republic sent for me. When he sent for anyone, it was rather serious; anything could happen, and no questions were asked or answered. You see, at that time, we were living under a dictatorship. Thank the Lord he was a good dictator. He cleaned up the country, although he took drastic measures to do so. Soon it was safe to travel where you wished and without fear. He placed competent men in each department. They, too, were dictators in their own domain, with authority to rule with an iron hand, which they did. This general had charge of the area where we lived. Living near to him, we knew him well, and, better still, he knew us very well.

Once while in conversation with him he told me that he liked me very much. He also liked our religion, but he would rather have the Roman Catholic religion because under it he could do as he liked. "You know, I do some very bad things," he said, "but I can take $5.00 over to the priests and all is forgiven. You cannot do that." "No," I said, "I cannot, but I can tell you of One who can, and you will not have to give Him $5.00, not even one cent."

When he sent for me, I went with mixed feelings. "Don Juan," he said, "I called for you to help me. I have three men here from the Mosquito District (Sambo Indians from Nicaragua). They say they are evangelists, but they are accused of some very bad things which, if guilty, may mean their death."

"I know you, and can put full confidence in you, but I do not know these men. I would like you to talk with them and let me know what you think of them. I do not want to punish innocent men, but if they are guilty, then they must be punished."

He told me they were accused of three things: cutting trees without permission, keeping men from their work, and receiving and obeying orders from a foreign country.

"Now," he said, "I will bring them in and you can take as long as you like to talk to them while I go to see to other things."

One of them I could truthfully say I knew, as I had met with him when I visited the Mosquito District years ago. He was sent over from Nicaragua from a mission there to start a work in Honduras. He arrived in Brus Lagoon (south of Trujillo) a few hours after I arrived. I asked him, after I was introduced to him, how he was going to start to make Christians out of these people. "We will invite all in the village to attend a special meeting," he said, "and all who wish we will baptize as Christians. Then, as babies are born into that family, we will baptize them as Christians." Of course, I did not agree with his answer and, naturally, I was saddened. Now, there I was once more in the presence of this man, along with two others I did not know.

I asked them why they cut down trees without permission. Their answer was they were told they had to go to Iriona and would get permission there. They had gone to Iriona and obtained written permission, which they now possessed. "What about keeping people from their work?" I then asked. They answered, "Every morning we ring a bell at 5 o'clock and the people come for prayer before starting work. In no way are we keeping them from work." "What about taking orders from a foreign country?" I finally asked. I suspected this was the real trouble. They explained that their bishop lived in Nicaragua, and every month he sent them orders as to what they were to do, where they were to go and what Scriptures they were to read.

Nicaragua and Honduras were at each other's throats at this time. Nicaragua had issued a postage stamp which showed a section of Honduras in Nicaragua and, of course, that did not go down well in Honduras.

I then saw the general and tried to explain their answers. I started with the tree cutting. I told him these men had written permission from Iriona to cut the trees necessary to build their houses. "Iriona has no authority to give this permission," the general told me. Then I said, "Are these men at fault for that, or is Iriona?" He had to agree that Iriona was at fault. About keeping the people from their work, he had to agree that they were only doing the same as the Roman Catholic Church.

I tried to explain that these men were only taking spiritual orders from their bishop who lived in Nicaragua. They were in no way receiving or obeying any kind of material orders from a foreign country. Well, I was not, I must confess, prepared for his reply to that.

"This is Trujillo," he said, "and I live in Trujillo, the head of the Mosquito District. I am the material man and I take all responsibility for material things. You also live in Trujillo. You are the spiritual man so you will take all responsibility for spiritual things in the future. You will tell these men and all others what they are to do and what they are not to do. You will be the bishop of the Mosquito District."

There you are, Bishop Ruddock. Did your heart ever jump to your mouth? Mine did. I said a hasty prayer to the Lord for wisdom, then a peaceful calm seemed to encircle me.

"General," I said, "that order is rather difficult for me to fulfil. I do not have anything to do with these men or their mission or their way of doing things." At this point, he cut me short. "You will in the future," he said. "You will give these men, and all others, orders as to spiritual conduct." Knowing the general as I did, I knew it would be useless to continue talking any further, so I said, "If you will allow me to take these men to my home for two weeks, I will have time to talk to them and explain all to them."

"That is what to do," he said. "Take them with you and explain that they are under your orders now." Almost four hours had passed since I left home and, of course, my wife Nettie and others were anxious to know what was wrong and if I was in any danger.

I talked to these three Sambo Indians and tried to explain as best I could how we obeyed the Scriptures in all spiritual things, but I found I might as well have been talking to the general. They were anxious to get back to their wives and children in the Mosquito District, as four months had passed since they had last seen them. I sent up much prayer concerning this matter. It was indeed very disturbing and was beginning to give me some severe migraine headaches.

Time was passing and I became more convinced that I must see the general again, so off I went. "General," I said, "I have two requests. Will you allow me to write to the mission headquarters (Moravian religion) of these men in the United States, stating the difficulties which have arisen here? I would like to petition them to send or appoint a bishop to live in Honduras so that no spiritual orders will be needed from Nicaragua or any other country." To my delight, he answered, "Yes, do that." The second request: "Can these men go home to their wives and children, as they have been away so long?" "They can," he replied, "so long as they are under your orders and take no orders from anyone else. If they do take orders from anyone else, they will be punished."

I, of course, explained this to the three men, telling them I could not give them spiritual orders because there was no authority for this in the Scriptures. I myself did not receive orders from anyone, nor did I give any orders, either. The Lord used the Holy Spirit and the Scriptures to guide and help in all spiritual matters. "Regarding material things, I would advise you to cut no more trees, build no more houses, and do not even send a letter to Nicaragua. I will write to your mission headquarters in the U.S.A. explaining the situation to them."

Off went the Sambo Indians to their homes and off went the letter I had said I would write. Soon I had a reply back thanking me for our kindness to their men and assuring me they understood the situation. A new bishop would be sent down to live in Honduras, thus overcoming the difficulty.

In a short time their new bishop did arrive. I took him down and introduced him to the general and to all the other officials he would have to deal with. The general made it very clear that I was in charge and everything had to pass through my hands. In fact, for a long time afterward, I had to interview all new missionaries coming to our part of the country and make things clear to them. This gave me a wonderful opportunity to see how far these missions were off the track and tell them the plain truths in God's Word as we learned them and practiced them.

One young couple came down with 10 boxes packed with stoves, washers, refrigerators and all kinds of cooking utensils only to stay for three weeks. They said it was not what they thought it would be like. Another young man came, fresh from some kind of religious school, and in conversation with him it was clear that he was really born again. "What are you going to do," I asked him, "when you go and settle down in this mission you have joined?" "Preach the gospel," he replied, "and pray that the Lord will save souls." "Are you sure?" I asked him. "Why yes, I am sure of that," he said, "that is why I came." "Well," I said, "I am not so sure. What will you do if you are told to baptize children to make them Christians?" "No, I could not do that," he said. "Well," I said, "I am afraid that is what you will have to do." "No, I won't," was his reply. "Who did you come here to work for?" I asked. "The Moravian mission," he said, mentioning their name. "They are responsible to give you the necessary money to live on?" "Yes," he said. "That is the difference between you and me," I told him. "I work for the Lord and He provides all I need, so I am free to preach the Gospel and do everything according to His instructions, but you are not."

Of course, he would not believe me. However, in a few weeks time I received a letter from him saying that it was as I had told him and he was retiring to look for a job elsewhere. I had an opportunity to talk with him some time later, but he could not take the step of trusting and depending on the Lord for guidance and support.

I came across another young man who passed through my hands. Years later I saw him again. "How are you?" I asked. "Very well health wise," he replied, "but spiritually I am not happy." "Why?" I asked. "The mission I work for," he told me, "sends a form for me to fill in every month. In this form there are many questions to be filled in, one is 'How many new Christians did you have during the month?' If I tell the truth and say 'None,' I get a letter back telling me to get busy. Each month I must be able to report quite a few conversions. Now I am not happy about that because many months pass without seeing anyone getting saved." Learn from this.

Many years after I had my encounters with the famous general, my wife was up in Tegucigalpa visiting one of the three Arabs she had nursed when they were sick with typhoid fever. This young lady had married, her husband passed away, and she was running her own business in the center of the city, a restaurant where light meals were served.

"Do you know who is in the restaurant?" she said to my wife. "The general." "I must go down to see him," Nettie replied, and off she went. When she entered, the general jumped to his feet and invited her to sit by him. He was so happy to see her again, as she had always been his favorite.

In the course of talking about old times, and the many awful things that had happened, he suddenly said, "Doña Nettie, do you think that there could be forgiveness for me? I have been guilty of many outrageous things." "Of course, general. The Lord Jesus Christ died on the cross and shed His precious blood so that you can be forgiven." She continued to talk to him and told him to look up some verses in the Bible. "But I do not have a Bible," he said. "I will get you a Bible," Nettie replied. "I am not returning to Tela, but I will get a Bible for you and leave it here in the restaurant where you can pick it up."

This she did, asking her friend to give it to the general when he came again. Not long after this, we heard he was found dead, kneeling on his bed in his room with the open Bible before him. Was that the last of this most famous general? We do not know any more details, but we do know if he really came to the Savior as a repentant sinner, and received by faith the Lord Jesus Christ, we will meet him in glory. What a day that will be.

# CHAPTER 30: Expatriates, Dreamers and Gold

In our travels, we came across another gentleman, an Englishman named Senior. He was living with an Irishman. These two men operated a banana plantation of their own. It wasn't very large, but they had operated it for some time. They also had some dairy cows. It takes about nine months after they're planted for bananas to be ready for marketing. So they made cheese and took it to Puerto Castillo to sell. In that way, they were able to keep themselves going while they waited on the bananas; however, sad to say, that was about the time that disease got into the bananas, and their business was not a success. These two men were more than middle-aged. The Irishman was a little older. I don't know much about their backgrounds. Senior had come out from England when he was young. He had traveled Central America quite a bit. Eventually, he settled in Honduras. He was a bachelor. He had gotten into contact with this Irishman, and they decided to try their hand in the banana business. We went out there and visited them on their farm, and always had an opportunity to tell them about the good news of salvation. Senior took quite an interest in it. We were able to explain to him in such a way that eventually he took his place as a sinner and received Christ as his Savior. He had opportunities to travel a little bit in his business as the Irishman wasn't able. He stayed at home and looked after the farm and the cattle, and did various other things about the place while his companion, Senior, went out and sold the milk, cheese and such like.

In one of these trips, Senior somehow got into contact with

one of the native women. That was his downfall. Evidently this
woman had been a kind of hypnotizer. She had a very bad influence over Mr. Senior. She could make him do whatever she
wanted. He spent some time at our home. And while there one
night he got up from his sleep and said that he had to go because this woman was calling for him. How he got that message
remains a mystery. I was away so my wife was alone. She had
great difficulty persuading him to go back to bed. It was maybe
2 o'clock in the morning. The train didn't leave until 6 in the
morning. Eventually he went back to bed. In the morning he returned to his own home. My wife found him one day in Puerto
Castillo in a very bad condition. He was all dirt and wet, in a
very bad state. He hardly knew what he was doing. We spoke to
the English consul about Senior, and he made arrangements for
him to be taken to the hospital. He was treated in the hospital
for some time. When he was released, he spent some time at
our house again. We tried to do the very best we could for him,
but it was rather difficult under the circumstances. It meant that
I had to stay at home to watch over him. He seemed to be getting worse. We made arrangements for him to be taken into the
hospital in La Ceiba.

Due to his bad condition, we decided to take him by airplane,
which were just starting in that part of the country. We finally
got up in the plane, but it was just a three-seater, with room for
only two passengers behind the pilot and the baggage. As soon
as we got up in the air, Senior opened the door of the plane. I
had to do some quick work to get a hold of him and push him
back into his seat. Fortunately, the door opened against the
wind, and the wind practically kept it closed. We got off the
plane and to the hospital, where he stayed for some little time.

By that time, the financial part of Senior's business with the
Irishman was rather low. The hospital was doing the very best
for him, but he needed medicine. I went out and saw his companion. He said, "Well, I don't know what we can do." He
blamed this Englishman for a whole lot of things. I said, "Be it
so, I don't know, but that's the condition he's in at the moment,
and he needs medicine." "Well," he said, "I could sell a couple
of cows." He did that, and with that money we were able to get
the medicine for Senior. He didn't live for so very long. He
passed away soon after. I believe, however, that he was a real
saved man, and he belonged to the Lord even though he had
this experience with this strange, bewitched woman.

One day, while I was passing out gospel tracts, I came to the house unexpectedly of the woman who was supposed to have hypnotized Senior. She invited me in for a cup of coffee, but I declined the invitation.

Another expatriate, Mr. Mac, came from the western part of the United States. He had been in Honduras for quite a long time. Many foreigners came to Honduras for various reasons, some had to flee the United States, while others came down on business. How he came down, we don't know. He traveled about quite a lot and tried his hand at various things. Gold mining was quite an attraction in Honduras. There has been money made on it. On the other hand, money has been lost. It's quite a risky venture. To go into it in a good, profitable way, one needs money and equipment. He did not have the luxury of those things. He might have panned a little gold to scratch out a living for a while, but he eventually got into the Carib Indian villages. There he established himself and made quite a lot of money by operating a little store. He had salt, sugar, groceries and things like that, even dry goods and potatoes. People bought material to make dresses and gentlemen's pants. He was the supplier for all of those things in some of the Carib Indian villages. He was able to make himself quite a good living and store up some money for the future. He knew quite a lot about these people, the Carib Indians. I myself learned a lot from him about them.

He came around to Trujillo while we were living there. We got to know him as our house there was the center for all foreign activities. Anyone who came from a foreign land somehow found our house. There was an open door for them always. There was something to eat, and we generally found a place for them to sleep. This dear man came along, and we took him in. When he came, he gave my wife a package to keep for him. Nettie thought it was ammunition or something like that because it was pretty heavy. She took that package, just threw it in among the soiled clothes and left it there by itself. He stayed for a couple of weeks or so. There was one thing my wife didn't like about him. When he came in, he would keep close to her. If she went to the kitchen, he followed her to the kitchen. If she went into the living room, there he was. He was always right beside her. He had quite a habit of sitting down close to whomever he was talking to. He made himself at home. Then the time came for him to leave. He asked my wife if she would very kindly go down with him to the train. He went a little early. Instead of going to the train, he got on the little boat that was going to one of the islands off the northern coast of Honduras. Eventually, he was going to Belize, British Honduras at that time. Before going, he asked my wife to kindly give him the money. She didn't remember him giving her any money. She said, "Money?" He said, "Yes. I gave you a package of money." Nettie was very much afraid, because she couldn't remember anything about money, but she did remember that he had given her a package and she knew where she'd put it. She went and got it for him. He said, "Yes, didn't you know, it's money?" There was the equivalent of thousands of dollars in gold, old gold and silver coins, and he was taking it with him. Evidently, he was leaving Honduras for good. At last, we found out why he kept so close to my wife. He was afraid that someone would do him harm. He was afraid that they were after him. We didn't know anything about that. He kept very close to her all the time. He used her as a safety guard. She was so well loved and respected that he knew no one would hurt her and that would protect him. He tried to keep as close to her as he could until he got onto the boat. Then he disappeared out of sight. That's the last we ever knew of him.

Among the other notables living around that part was a man by the name of Stephenson. He lived way in the backwoods, in the jungle. He had a little shack that he made himself. He was accustomed to sit at his door with a gun across his knees. He would simply lift the gun if anyone tried to get near him and that was enough warning. They would make a hasty retreat out of his sight. Evidently he didn't care about neighbors or company. There were others, too. In fact, Honduras in the bygone days was quite a place for those who were fleeing from the law. The first time I heard of Tegucigalpa, or Honduras, was way back in the year 1921 or '22 in Los Angeles. The circumstance was over a lady who had killed another lady. It was known in the media as the hammer murder. A Mrs. Philips was captured and put in prison. She escaped when someone smuggled her a rope. Eventually they found her in Tegucigalpa. A Los Angeles sheriff was sent down to get her. He went to Tegucigalpa and brought her home. His wife went along with him. While there, she contracted some kind of a tropical disease that caused her death.

Another expatriate we ran into in Trujillo was a doctor. He was quite a writer at the same time. He wrote a book. He had my wife revise it and go over it for him. It was, indeed, rather interesting. It told quite a lot about the country and about ambushes and revolutions. When it was ready, he sent it off to be printed, but he could find no one to print it. The trouble was that he didn't have enough excitement between women and men in it. That's what the public wants. They would rather satisfy the flesh than the spirit. The publisher wrote him a nice letter back saying that the book was wonderful, but it needed more lovemaking in it. But this doctor wasn't interested in that kind of book, and eventually it was put to one side and there was nothing more done about it. This doctor also did some gold mining, but I don't think he was any more successful in that.

It took a lot of money to go into the gold business. Of course, there were men that eked out a living just for themselves and nothing more. They would sift the sand along the river banks and find enough gold perhaps for a day's wages, but that's about all. In fact, a man who lived in Tela, would go out on a trip every once in a while. He was very, very secretive about those trips, but he would come home with enough gold to get him along for a little while longer. He would make his way up the mountains and come onto these places and bring back a little gold. Another doctor also came down from the U.S. to try gold mining. His son told me that if his father had all the money that he had spent on the machinery and the men's wages and everything else, he'd be quite a rich man. He, too, was unable to make a success of it. Sadly, too many of these expatriates ignored the spiritual things and died slaves to the flesh.

# CHAPTER 31: General Christmas and the Monkey General

We never did know General Christmas, but we were very well-acquainted with some who knew him very well. This man worked in the railroad business in New Orleans. He was a driver on the passenger and freight trains that went out from New Orleans. He was color blind and when a new law came in that no color blind person could be employed as an engineer, he lost his job. He made his way down Central America to Honduras. There it didn't matter whether one was color blind or not. He got a job with the National Railroad. It went from Puerto Cortes up to San Pedro Sula and on to Porteriolles.

A revolution broke out on this particular day. He got the train only a few blocks, but could get no further because of the revolution. The government forces and the opposition army were there, blocking the way. They weren't fighting, but they weren't getting on very well, either. Christmas thought that he could help them. He got the ice out of the ice car. The company had an ice factory then in Puerto Cortes. In those days there was no refrigeration. Even for business, they used ice quite a lot. He used the ice as a kind of fortress and got one of the soldiers to lend him his gun. He got behind the ice and persuaded the others to follow him. There they were behind this barricade of ice, which proved to be quite a fortress, and then they began shooting. Pretty soon they had chased away the enemy. The soldiers saw the possibilities of having this man go along with them and be their leader. Right there on the spot they made him their general. He became General Christmas ever after that, but he didn't want to go. He said, "My job is finished now. I want to get to San Pedro with the train. That's my real business. This thing got

in my way, but now I want to get there." They said, "Look
here, you're in it as well as us now. You helped us and now
they'll be after you. If you don't look out for yourself, you're
going to be severely punished. In some way perhaps you'll lose
your life." At last they did convince Christmas to go along with
them. He went as General Christmas.

When they got to San Pedro Sula, he gave the orders and they
soon gained the barracks in San Pedro Sula. They now controlled practically the whole north coast of Honduras. Then they
went on into the interior. They were moving with more force
and power now, winning victory after victory. Finally, they
marched right into the capital Tegucigalpa. With his followers,
he took the barracks there. They proclaimed him the general of
all the forces. However, he wasn't really a political man, so after
everything got quiet again, he went back to Puerto Cortes. He
liked to live there. He became quite a help for the country in
many ways. Which side was he on? I don't know. Those days
there was the Red party and the Blue party. If the party in
power changed, you had better change your tie. When the Red
party was in, you'd better wear a red tie, but if the Blue party
was back in power that morning, you had to be pretty quick on
the draw to get your tie changed.

On and off he helped his party. At last his party lost power
and he had to flee. He went into hiding, and finally escaped the
country. He escaped under very strange circumstances. A dear
woman that we knew very well helped him in La Ceiba. Fruit
boats sailed up to New Orleans and to other international ports
from La Ceiba. She fixed him up in women's clothing, even with
a hat. It happened to be in the rainy season, so they waited until
the rain was pretty heavy, and went out and walked with their
umbrellas quite low to the docks past the guards. This woman
and General Christmas walked side by side. They went to the
boat and very boldly got on the ladder and on the boat. This
dear woman left him there. She perhaps saved his life. Those
things were not uncommon down there. That woman herself
was quite a character. She had one left finger blown off by a revolver at one time.

General Ardonas was another man who was quite well known
in his day. He was quite a general, too. He came through a
number of wars – revolutions, of course. He had been in a few
narrow escapes. Indeed, the first time I met him he was convalescing from some wounds he had received. He was sitting in a
chair one day when I went around to his house passing out gos-

pel tracts. He asked me to come up and sit by his side. I did so, and he gave me quite an outline of his life. One time he was taken prisoner by the soldiers to Puerto Cortes. They were watching him there in a special house that they had. He made an excuse that he had to go to the rest room. When he got to the rest room, he saw a very small hole in the roof. He got himself pulled up to it and out onto the roof, where he found that he could travel for quite a distance. Off he went along the roofs of many houses, and had a little jumping to do, back and forth like a monkey at times. He kept this up until he thought that he was far enough away to escape. He got down and made his way down to the beach. Puerto Cortes is one of the ports of Honduras. There were always quite a few boats there. There were some very small boats called *cayucos*. They were just sufficient for one or two men. He took possession of one of these boats and found himself a kind of an oar. He rowed and rowed until he thought he was far out of sight of the beach. He struggled along as best he could. He eventually got away out in the Caribbean and drifted for a few days.

No one missed him for some little time in the place where he was imprisoned. At last, when they did, it was too late. They couldn't make out where he had gone. They looked all over and couldn't find him. By this time, he was drifting out into the ocean. He tried to make out he was a fisherman in the hope that a boat would come along and pick him up, but that didn't happen. He drifted there for a long time. He couldn't come near the shore because he was afraid he would get caught. Eventually he came to a place near Belize. He landed on the beach there. He found something to eat and located some friends.

Pretty soon he was strong enough to travel again. By that time, his party had taken power in Honduras. He could safely return to Honduras, again. During some other disturbances in Honduras he got shot up, and that's when I found him convalescing. I had quite a conversation with him, and found that he was very much interested in spiritual things. At one time he had been contacted by Adventists. He wanted to know about their doctrine, and he wanted to know about what the Scriptures taught. I was able to explain those things to him. Eventually that dear man received Christ as his Savior. Soon he was able to be about his business again. He lived for some time in Trujillo. In fact, he was baptized there and received into the meeting. He was quite a little help there for some time, and he gave a good testimony.

# CHAPTER 32: Left-Armed Samson

One of the elders of the Progreso assembly (a city near the north coast of Honduras) would not take that title. He would tell you he is unworthy. He would tell you he is only a sinner saved by grace, seeking to help his Lord, His work and His people. And that's just what he is doing. He has only one arm, the left arm, and he has many scars all over his face – all over his body, in fact. Why? What happened? Left-Armed Samson was caught in a family feud. Feuds are common in that part of Honduras. Families get divided for some reason or other, and once in awhile they will make a raid on each other. They take their machetes along with them, and therefore there's some blood shed. Many times lives are taken. In the family of Left-Armed Samson, the feud had gone on for many years. They had already lost to violence some of their family on both sides. On this occasion, the other side of the family came suddenly upon Left-Armed Samson's family, and there was a slaughter. Two brothers and the father were killed outright. Left-Armed Samson was also very badly wounded, cut up by the machetes. One arm was cut off altogether. He had many wounds on his legs, body and face; however, he must have been a rather strong young man, and he survived. Somehow he got the bleeding stopped, got to a place of shelter and recovered his strength again.

He now knew what he had to do. There were only two members of the opposing family left. It was his duty to avenge his family. He left his village and went down to the coast. He found a job with the fruit company, using a machete to cut bananas. He practiced there for two years, practiced cutting all kinds of material. Not only the bananas, but grass and trees. He practiced until he got good strength in that left arm. He had wonderful strength in it, and he knew it was time to go and look these two men up. It took him some time to find out where these brothers were. When he found them, it came rather quickly and unexpectedly. He was walking along a narrow path when suddenly who should turn the corner but these two brothers. He got quite a fright. The two brothers didn't realize who they were facing at first. Samson had only one arm, and a left arm at that, to face them with, but he had spent time getting his machete and arm in good shape. There they were, two against one. He didn't know what to do. He hadn't expected to take the two on at one time, but how could he let this opportunity pass? He started in, and what a fight it was, blow after blow. He had turned from one to the other until one of the brothers went down. Then Samson went right after the other one until he went down, too. He made sure that they were both dead, really dead, because he remembered that they thought they had left him dead. He had avenged his family.

All of the opposing family in the feud were dead; all of his family were dead. There was none but himself, so he turned back down to the coast. He found work in another banana farm, but this farm was a little different than the other. There were some Christians in this one, and, of course, they were very active. Out they would go at night with their Coleman lamp, preaching the gospel. That was something very new for our Left-Armed Samson. He listened to the gospel, and he came back night after night. Soon his sins began to trouble him as he heard the message of God's word. God loves the sinner but hates the sin, those dear men in the camp kept preaching. Poor Left-Armed Samson was in distress, until he finally took his place as a sinner and received Christ as his Savior. Thank the Lord for that. He was now a new man in Christ Jesus. Yes, Left-Armed Samson was indeed a new creature in Christ Jesus. He would have liked to have washed the wounds that he had inflicted upon those two men, but that was an impossibility. They were gone, already buried. Somehow that kept this poor man in agony. After God saved him, he realized the depth of sin that he had been in and that disturbed him very much. He could have no peace of mind. He couldn't settle down to anything. He wanted to be of a help, but these thoughts would fill his mind and his heart. He spoke to the other Christians in the camp about this. He came to the conclusion that the only way he could find relief was to turn himself in and confess what he had done to these two men.

He left the camp, went back to the village up in the mountains and lost no time in telling authorities what he had done. It appears that they looked upon him as some man that was a little bit touched in the head. They had never met anyone that would tell them that he had killed two men and ask to be punished for it. They looked in the criminal records of murders for the year. His name wasn't there. They scoured the criminal records for other dates, but nothing showed up. He had committed no crime. They came to the conclusion that instead of coming to see them he should have gone to see a doctor. At last they said, "No, there's nothing against you." Still Samson stood there, and they wondered what kind of man he was. Again they said, "Look here. There's nothing against you. You're a free man. Go back home. Go to the place that you came from and work as you ought to do." At last it sunk in. He had tried, but in the eyes of the law of the land he was a free man. I expect a revolution had occurred near that time and there were things more important for the authorities to do than to look for a man that only killed two men.

Back Samson went to the coast, and the Christians were waiting for him. They had been praying while he was away. The outcome had satisfied them, and it seemed to satisfy Samson as well. Now his conscience was clear. He had done all that was in his power to confess to the authorities what he had done, but they had sent him away a free man. God had forgiven him his sins, and as far as the country was concerned he was forgiven also. Left-Armed Samson began to help the dear Christian men who were there proclaiming the good news of salvation in the camp in which he lived and in other camps around. He grew in grace and in knowledge of the Lord Jesus Christ. He was very good at conferences, a popular gospel preacher. Having his experience, he knew how to speak to them in a very clean, frank language. God used him.

# CHAPTER 33: Distributing the Gospels Door to Door

It was my privilege and a great opportunity to distribute the gospels (Matthew, Mark, Luke and John) right from the border of Guatemala, along the north coast of Honduras, to the border of Nicaragua. I had some wonderful times during those early days.

On one occasion I visited one of the Carib Indian villages. As usual, I went from house to house, leaving a little gospel in each house. I followed that up later with another gospel and another gospel until each house had all four. I would also provide New Testaments and complete Bibles for anyone who showed great interest. This day, I was going from one house to another when I looked back and saw a man who seemed to be following me. He was getting nearer and nearer. When he was right up to me, he said, "Excuse me, I would like you to come down to my home. I have something there I would like to ask you about." "With much pleasure," I said. I went with him to his little hut, and there he brought out a Bible. He asked me, "Is this a good Bible? I would like to know that." I looked at it, and said it was a good Bible all right. I assured him of that fact. "Well," he said, "it tells the truth, doesn't it?" "Yes," I said, "it tells the truth." "Then," he said in a rather mournful voice, "I'm a condemned man." He had discovered through reading the Bible on his own that he was a condemned man. And, of course, that troubled him. I asked him why he thought he was condemned. "Well," he said, "according to what I read here in this book, and according to how I have lived, I have sinned and disobeyed God. And it tells me here that there's punishment for a life like that." I said, "You are right. That's very true."

We went on speaking together for some considerable time. I brought the Scriptures before him. Eventually, that very evening before I left, he was rejoicing in the knowledge that his sins had been forgiven, and that there was no more condemnation for him. I left him, but in three months I was back again. I tried to make that trip every three months, until I had the four gospels given to each of the dear people. When I went back the second time, I still found him rejoicing in the knowledge that all his sins had been taken care of through the death and punishment of the Lord Jesus Christ for him on the cross. There was something else troubling this dear man. God had only one way of saving a sinner, only one. It does not matter what part of the world you are in. It's the experience that is different. Nearly all experiences before anyone receives Christ as his Savior are very different. And, as a rule, their experiences afterwards are different, too. He said, "Will you do something for me?" "With the greatest of pleasure," I answered. I'm always very obliging, you know. He said, "There's something I want you to see." He went into another room and brought out a package.

He began to open that package. It took him some considerable time. It was well wrapped. It was wrapped the way that we made a football when we were boys, wrapped with pieces of paper, string, cord, socks and all kinds of wool shirts. He had this wrapped just like that. At last, it was getting smaller and smaller until it was so small I thought there must be nothing in it at all. He took the last wrapping off and then took it out. It was a little chain. On the end of that little chain was the image of the Virgin Mary. He said, "Here's what's troubling me. Since I received Christ as my Savior, I have no use for this, but it's in the house and it troubles me. What can I do now? What will I do with this?" I knew what he was hinting at because it takes someone some considerable time after being saved before he can throw out all that which he had confidence and faith in before. I said, "Well, there are several things you could do with it. You could throw it in the river down there or you could give it to me and I'll take care of it for you." "Would you take it?" he asked. "Yes," I said, "with pleasure." "Here you are," he said as he handed it to me. What a load that was off his heart. He revived again. He showed more life. There were many more like him, too.

# CHAPTER 34: The Carib Indians

The Carib Indians living on the north coast of Honduras are very peaceable, lovable people; yet there is a certain hidden mystery about them. It is supposed that they offered up human sacrifices to their deities at an annual secret feast. This I often wondered about as I worked with the Carib Indians over the years. But it was difficult to get any substantial information about such feasts. By reading Sydney Watson's book, *In the Twinkling of An Eye*, I came across a very interesting account of their feasts. In his Revell book, Mr. Watson mentions two men, Ralph Bastin and a Mr. Hammond. It appears Bastin had been away on an extended trip, and when he came home he related to his friend Hammond something of his experiences while on the island of Utila. Utila is one of three islands several miles off the Honduran coast. The British landed many Carib Indians there after finding they had killed governors which the English had left to look after their interests on the island of Grenada and other British West Indian islands. We will now join Bastin telling Hammond about one of the Carib Indian feasts which he attended secretively. I quote:

"I have told you hurriedly something of where I have been," Bastin began. "But I have reserved my great story until I could tell it to you here." He glanced down at the child at his feet. "I heard," he went on, "when at La Caribe – as everyone hears who stays long in the place – that each year, in spite of the laws of the whites, who are in power, a child is sacrificed to the Carib deities, and I longed to know if it were true."

"During my first few week's sojourn on the little island of Utila, I was able to render one of the old priests a service, which somehow became so exaggerated in his eyes that there was almost literally nothing that he would not do for me, and eventually he yielded to my entreaties to give me a chance to see for myself the yearly sacrifice, which was due in a month's time.

"During that month of waiting I made many sketches of this wonderful neighborhood, and became acquainted with this little Carib maiden, painting her in three or four different ways. The child became intensely attached to me, and I to her, and we were always together in the daytime.

"As the time drew near for the sacrifice, I noticed that the little one grew very elated, and there was a new flash in her eyes, a kind of rapturous pride. I asked her no question as to this change, putting it down as girlish pride on being painted by the 'white prince,' as she insisted on calling me.

"I need not trouble you, my dear fellow, with unnecessary details of how and where the old priest led me on the eventful night, which was as black as Erebus, but come to the point where the real interest begins.

"It was midnight when at last I had been smuggled into that mysterious cave, which, if only a tithe of what is reported be half true, has been damned by some of the awfullest deeds ever perpetrated. My priest-guide made me swear, before starting, that whatever I saw I would make no sign, utter no sound, telling me that if I did, and we were discovered, we should both be murdered there and then.

"We had hardly hidden ourselves before the whole center of the cave became illuminated with a colored flame that burned up from a flat brass brazier, and seemed like the colored fires used in pantomime effects on the English stage. By this wonderful light I saw 150 or more Carib men and women file silently into the cave and take up their positions in orderly rows all round the place. When they had all mustered, a sharp note was struck upon the carimba, a curious one-stringed instrument, and the circles of silent savages dropped into squatting position on their heels. Then the weirdest of all weird music began, the instruments being a drum, a flute and the carimba.

"But my whole attention became absorbed by the grouping in the center of the room – the fire-dish had been shifted to one side, and I saw a hideous statue, squatted on the rudely constructed, massive table, the carved hands gripping a bowl that rested on the stone knees of the image. The head of the hideous god was encircled with a very curious band, that looked, from where I stood, like bead and grass and feather work. The face – cheeks and forehead – was scored with black, green and red paint, the symbolic colors of the wondrous race that once filled all Central America.

"In the back part of the wide, saucer-like edge of the bowl which rested on the knees of the statue, there burned a light-blue flame, and whether it was from this fire, or from the larger one that burned in the wide, shallow brazier on the floor, I cannot positively say, but a lovely fragrance was diffused from one or the other.

"Before this strange altar stood three very old priests, while seven women (*sukias*), as grizzled as the men, stood at stated intervals about the altar. One of these hideous hags had a dove in her hand; another held a young kid clasped between her strong brown feet; a third held the sacrificial knife, a murderous-looking thing, made of volcano glass, short in blade, and with a peculiar jagged kind of edge; another of these hags grasped a snake by the neck – a blood-curdling-looking *tamagas*, a snake as deadly as a rattle-snake.

"Opposite the center-man of the three old priests stood a girl-child, about 10 years of age, and perfectly nude. During the first few moments the vaporous kind of smoke that was wafted by a draught somewhere from the fire-pan on the floor of the cave hid the child's features, though I could see how beautiful of form she was; then, as the smoke-wreath presently climbed straight up, I was startled to see that the child was my little friend.

"In my amazement I had almost given vent to some exclamation, but my old priest-guide was watching me, and checked me.

"My little one's beautiful head was wreathed with jasmine, and a garland of purple *madre-de-cacao* blossoms hung about her lovely shoulders.

"Suddenly, like the barely audible notes of the opening music of some orchestral number, the voice of one of the priests began to change; in turn, the two other priests took up the strain; then each of the seven hags in their turn, and then each in the first circle of squatting worshipers, followed by each woman in the second row: and in this order the chant proceeded, until, weird and low, every voice was engaged.

"Suddenly the combined voices ceased, and one woman's voice alone rose upon the stillness; and following the sound of the voice, I saw that it was the mother of my little native child-friend. I had not noticed her before – she had been squatting out of sight. Hers was not the chant of the others, but a strange, mournful wail. It lasted about a minute-and-a-half; then, rising to her feet, she gently thrust the child forward towards the altar, then laid herself face down on the floor of the cave.

"The little one leaned against the edge of the altar, and taking up, with a tiny pair of bright metal tongs, a little fire out of the back edge of the bowl on the knees of the god, she lit another fire on the front edge of the bowl, her suddenly illuminated face filled with a glowing pride.

"Then, at a signal from the head priest, the child lifted her two hands, extended them across the altar, when they were each seized by the two other priests, and the beautiful little body was drawn slowly, gently, over, until the smooth breast almost touched the sacrificial fire she had herself lit.

"Then I saw the woman who had held the knife suddenly yield it up to the head priest, and I made an unconscious movement to spring forward.

"My guide held me, and whispered his warning in my ear; yet even though I must be murdered myself, I felt I dared not see that sweet young life taken.

"Like a man suffering with nightmare, who wants to move, but cannot, I stood transfixed, fascinated, one instant longer. But in that flashing instant the head priest had swept with lightning speed, the edge of that hideous knife twice across the little one's breast, and she stood smiling upwards like one hypnotized.

"The priest caught a few drops of the child's blood, and shook them into the bowl of the god; then I saw the little one fall into her mother's arms; there was a second sudden flashing of that hideous knife, a piteous, screaming cry, and I gave vent to a yell – but not voice to it – for the watching guide at my side clapped one hand tightly over my mouth, while with the other he held me from flying out into the ring of devils, whispering in my ear as he held me back.

" 'It is the goat that is slain, not the child.'

"Another glance, and I saw that this was so; one flash of that obsidian sacrificial blade across the throat of the kid had been enough, and now the blood was being drained into the bowl of the god.

"I need not detail all the other hideous ceremonies; they lasted for nearly two hours longer, ending with a mad frenzied dance, in which all joined save the priests and the mother and child.

"Every dancer, man and woman, flung off every rag of clothing, and whirled and leaped and gyrated in their perfect nudity, until, utterly exhausted, one after another they sank upon the floor.

"Then slowly they gathered themselves up, reclothed themselves and left the cave. And now some large pine torches were lighted, and my guide drew me further back, that the increased glare might not reveal our presence, and I saw the curious ending to this weird night's work. The priests and their seven women *sukias* opened a pit in the floor of the cave by shifting a great slab of stone, and lowered the idol into the pit. The remains of the kid, the sacrificial knife, and the dove were dropped into the bowl of blood that rested on the knees of the idol; then the sukia that had held the tamagas snake during the whole of those hideous night hours, dropped the writhing thing into the bowl, and the slab was lowered quickly over the pit, every seam around the slab being carefully filled, and the whole thing hidden by sprinkling loose dust and the ashes from the fire over the spot.

"Then, as soon as the last of the performers had cleared the cave, I followed my guide, and with a throbbing head, and full of a sense of strange sickness, I went to the house where I was staying.

"I lay down upon my bed, but could not sleep; and as early as I dared I went round to my little Martarae's home – Martarae was her native name. Her mother met me, said that the child would not come out in the sun today, that I might see her for a moment if I pleased, but that she was not very well.

"Sweet little soul! I found her lying on her little bed, with a proud light in her eyes, and a very flushed face.

"A fortnight later the light flesh wounds were healed. She showed me her breast, confided to me the story, and asked me if I did not think she had much to be proud of.

" 'Will you keep a secret?' I asked her. She gave me her promise, and I told her how I had seen the whole thing, and all my fears for her.

"A week later she was orphaned. Her mother was stung by a deadly scorpion, and died in an hour, and I made the child my care.

"She has traveled everywhere with me ever since, and you see how fair and sweet she is, and how beautifully she speaks our

English. She is barely 12, is naturally gifted, and is the very light of my life."

"Would she let me see her breast, Ralph, do you think?" Hammond asked.

Bastin smiled, and spoke a word to the child, and she, rising to her feet and smiling back at him, unfastened the broach at her throat, and, laying back her breast-covering, showed the gleaming, shiny scars. Then as she recovered her chest, she said softly:

"Ralph has taught me those gods were evil; but though I shall ever wear this cross in the flesh of my breast, I shall ever love the Christ who died on the world's great cross at Calvary."

"It is a most marvelous story, Ralph," he said tearing his eyes away from the child's clear, searching gaze.

"The more marvelous because absolutely true," returned Bastin.

What I'd often wondered about this story was later confirmed by an old American from Walla Walla, Washington. I found him in one of these Carib Indian Villages while I was distributing the gospels from door to door. He told me a little about his own life, about how he came to be there and how he had lived for many years among these dear people. He made his living in their villages by selling them the necessities of life: clothing, material to make dresses, shirts, belts and such like. He also sold salt, sugar and other things that they liked to get. He was able to make a good living out of that. That poor man though had no interest at all in eternal things. But, thank the Lord, I found among those dear Caribs much interest and some of them were saved by the grace of God. We found work among the Carib Indians unpredictable but very, very interesting.

After the assembly in Aguan was started, I traveled further afield to the far away Carib Indian villages. To get to them we found we could take the train part way and then walk, or sometimes it was possible to take a canoe where there was a canal. Occasionally on these trips we found very, very much interest in spiritual things and other times not so much.

For example, upon arriving at a little Indian village called Battalia there was a young man who professed to be saved. His name was Don Vicente. At that village he would come along and lend a helping hand. We found him very useful and helpful. While visiting those villages it's no use arriving in the morning.

You'll find the village deserted. The men folk have gone to fish and the women folk have gone more inland planting and tending their casabas. So, if you arrived in the morning, you have to pass through that village and keep walking on until you come to a village in the afternoon, and there you can start to work.

When I got to Battalia on this morning, Vicente was ready and he came along with me. When we arrived at the next village, we went into a home that we had entered before. We wanted to get a drink and then go to another village further on where the people had already returned from their work. On this occasion though, Vicente and the lady of the house seemed to have quite a talk. The lady of the house was a little excited. Of course, you know, they speak their own language, as well as the Spanish language. So she was speaking to Vicente in their own language. At last, I asked Vicente, "Does there seem to be anything wrong?" He said, "Yes, the priest was here last week, and he gave orders that no one was to help us in any way. They weren't to give us any food, any water, or help to get to the next village." "Well," I said. "It's time we were going anyhow. So let's go." We went out through the door and turned around to find a path just when the man of the house came along. "Oh, Don Juan," he said. "I thought you were never coming back. What kept you? Why were you so long? Come right in." "Well," Vicente said, "sorry, but how can we go in? We have just been put out?" So Vicente explained to him what had happened. "Come on in," he said. "I'm the head of my own house. The priest has nothing to say here. He comes around when the women folk are alone, and he can do what he likes with them. Come on in." So we went in. He was very anxious to know, as they nearly all were, how much we charged to baptize a child? That was foremost in his mind because they really did not have the money to pay for such a thing. That gave me, of course, an opportunity to explain something about baptism.

So I turned him to the Scriptures. And, do you know what? I was so involved in speaking to him that when I finally looked up I counted six men sitting on their heels around the wall of the room. Pretty soon more came in, and that encouraged me to keep on talking. I talked for over three hours without stopping. And they listened while I explained about baptism; what it was, who it was for, and of course, emphasizing that those who have freely received shall freely give. That was quite an exciting afternoon as we stayed there for so long. The fact of the matter is we could hardly get away from that village.

In another village the Caribs had gotten the same orders from a priest. We tried to get a few to listen to the message, but they said we couldn't be there. I said at the last, "Supposing that we stay outside of the house. How would that do?" "Oh, that would be all right. The priest hadn't said anything about the outside of the house. It was only the inside." "Very good then." I told the dear people there that when the sun went down (because there were no clocks there), I would be outside at a certain place to explain many things. "Will you come along?" I said. When the sun began to set, they came, from all parts. Some carried three-legged stools; others, chairs; still others, boxes to sit on. And there we had quite a meeting. The Lord used his word in many of those Carib villages. We thank the Lord for that. That was the object of our being there in the first place, of course. We would have been very content to have remained in that part of the country and continue with that work, but it was not to be.

We were sitting one morning in Tela, enjoying our breakfast at about seven o'clock. Everyone down in the tropics gets up early. The cocks begin to crow, and the girls come along shouting, selling oranges, *N-a-r-a-n-j-a-s*, or coconut, *C-o-c-o-s*. And, of course, with all that noise, and with the heat at the same time, it's more comfortable to get up. You just wake up along with all the others. It's more comfortable to get out of bed. Everything opens up at eight o'clock in the morning, and they all try to get their business done before the heat of the day really commences. So we were enjoying our breakfast when something unusual happened. Don Vicente came to the door. He is the one who had traveled with us to various Carib Indian villages over the years. In Tela, and on both sides of Tela, there were two or three Carib Indian villages. Vicente had been having Bible meetings in those villages. Now he seemed to be very excited. The natural color of those people's skin is kind of brown, darkish brown. Some are darker than others. However, Vicente's face that morning was a sickly green kind of color, the poor fellow. It was easy to see that something unusual had happened.

"What's the matter, Vicente?" I said. "Ohhh, Don Juan. What a night." When the meeting had ended, he went to bed where he was staying.

At about two o'clock in the morning, soldiers came around and took all the men down to the *playa*, the beach. They lined them up there, and the soldiers had their rifles. The head man gave the orders, and bang, down went the first Carib Indian.

That command was repeated two or three times, and down went others. They were coming very near Vicente, but there was one of the governing people, a mixture of Spanish and Indian blood about sixth down the line of men, and before Don Vicente.

The government in power was the Blue party, and the opposition party was Red, but they were all members of that mixed Spanish and Indian race. The Red and Blue parties were in a constant struggle. The Reds wanted back in power again, and it appears that their soldiers had been out of the country somewhere and come back in little boats near this village. There was a river there, and they were able to sail this river. They had gotten way up near the interior of the country before the Blue government was alerted to what was happening. They captured the Red soldiers finally, but blamed the people in this Carib Indian village for helping them to get in. "Where were they?" they said. "Why didn't they see them and notify the government?" The Blue party's idea was to shoot and kill a few of the Carib Indians to frighten the living daylights out of the Red Party so that they would confess what had happened. When the Blue soldiers got near one of these Red party members, they gave the orders to stop shooting. They called this man to one side, which caused a little confusion, naturally, and Vicente and some of the others took the opportunity to turn on their heels and run.

Vicente never stopped until he got up to our house. That is often the extent of human rights down there. That cultural conflict is troubling the people to this day. Maybe one day they'll get things settled. It's difficult for Americans to understand. However, we would have gladly given all our lives to those dear Carib Indian people while we were in Trujillo, but circumstances wouldn't allow us to stay. The banana business had suffered a colossal failure. A disease crept in and destroyed the crops so that the companies weren't able to carry on. Banana plantations in that part of the country were shut down completely. That meant that all the Christians, and nearly all the men living around Trujillo, had to go and look for work somewhere else. There was no train. They even lifted the rails. There was no communication and no transportation. In those days they were just getting the airlines into shape, but they were very dear (expensive) at that time which wouldn't permit one such as a missionary to use them often. So everybody left Trujillo. I counted 60 believers who had been part of our lives while we were there, and they had all gone to other places.

And because of this exodus there was great need then in another part of the country. After we moved to Tela, we again had transportation to take us anywhere but if we had remained in Trujillo, we would have been shut in. You'd have to walk anywhere. Walking is wonderful too, but when it comes to 60 miles at a stretch, that's a different thing. So we moved on the coast north to Tela. We had a lot of work afterward in Tela and in that vicinity. Up to that time there were very few other missionaries who had come to help, but about that time more came. We now had the help of James Scollon and his wife from Detroit. And, of course, the Carib Christians themselves carried on very well.

## Notes on attending services near Tela:

Since returning, I have been making it a point to visit some of the newer and rural assemblies on the Lord's Day. I have found this a good idea as many of the believers who work on the banana farms, etc., or because of distance, are only able to attend the meetings on Sundays. I generally remain in Tela one Sunday in the month, and then visit different assemblies the other three Sundays.

The following is an account of the past month's work on the Lord's days:

The first Sunday in November I visited the small assembly in Las Palmas. This is not a new assembly, but is of many years standing. It has not grown much, perhaps because of its location and sparse population, but it gives us joy to see the few believers go on faithfully for God. This place is just three-quarters of an hour ride by bicycle and then another three-quarters of an hour's walk from Tela. During the wet season it is impossible to use the bicycle as the road in parts is under water. The remembrance feast began at noon with 10 believers gathered around the table. This was followed by a ministry meeting when we sought to encourage these dear believers to go on for Christ. After a short visit, I left for Tela again and the gospel meeting there in the evening.

The second Sunday the alarm clock went off at 4 a.m. This gave me time to get ready, have some coffee and walk to the station to catch the train leaving at 5 a.m. I arrived at Uluita, a

201

small rural settlement at 6:30 a.m. The breaking of bread meeting began at 9 a.m. when 25 believers gathered to remember the Lord. Four hymns were sung, eight brethren led in prayer, and one brother read from the Scriptures. It was a precious time. At one o'clock there was a ministry meeting, and a few believers from the assembly in Agua Blanca had walked the four miles from there to be at this meeting. The hall was well filled. This hall was built by the brethren themselves, and has a thatched roof, rough, hand sawed board sides, and railroad ties which had been discarded by the fruit company for a floor. Many questions were asked and answered between meetings and at 4:30 p.m. when the train, which had taken us there in the morning, returned and took us back to Tela by 6:30 p.m. just in time for the gospel meeting there.

On the third Sunday, there was no need for the alarm clock for I stayed in Tela. The breaking of bread is at 9 a.m. and that particular Lord's day 40 met to remember the Lord, and almost as many as that sat back. It is surprising how many people came into the hall at Tela to see how we remember the Lord. Immediately after the breaking of bread meeting, we have Sunday school. This was open Sunday because I was at home. The other Sundays the school is divided into classes. We find the Sunday school is coming up in numbers since our return. In the afternoon there was the prison and hospital work and visiting, the women's Bible class 5:30 p.m., and the gospel meetings at 7 p.m. A native brother always shares this meeting, and some of them give a very fine message.

The fourth Sunday, the alarm clock did not forget to go off at 4 a.m. and by 5 a.m. I was on the train and en route for Bataan, a large hemp farm where there is a fine new assembly. I traveled on this train until 9:30 a.m. and then transferred to a branch line. Our coach on this line was an old cattle wagon with hard seats on either side and one running up the middle of the car. One hour's ride brought us back to Bataan. The morning meeting (communion service) began at 11 a.m. here and 16 met to remember the Lord while three believers who are not yet in fellowship sat back. Immediately after the morning meeting, there was a ministry meeting, and we had the privilege of speaking on the Lord's Supper. I did not have much opportunity to visit with the Christians at this place since I had to be back to the cattle wagon by 1:30 p.m. so as to get out on the main line and be back in Tela for the gospel meeting at night. When I left, some of the brethren were busy with the Sunday school and others were planning to go with tracts to another farm a few miles away.

We arrived at the main line to find the train was late, a not uncommon happening. As I boarded the train when it did come, I could hear the sound of angry voices in a heated argument. Suddenly one of these men drew his revolver and was going to settle the argument with it. This was the sign for most of the passengers to jump from their seats and rush into the next coach. Someone must have persuaded him to pocket his pistol again for everything became quiet. About half an hour later three shots rang out from a revolver just two seats in front of me, and this caused some of the most nervous passengers to jump again, but they soon settled down when someone shouted out that they were only shooting at a monkey on one of the trees as the train passed. Later on in the evening two more shots rang out from behind me, and again some of the passengers jumped, but it was only someone trying his pistol out through the window. By 6:30 p.m. we were in Tela and, after a hasty wash up and a cup of coffee, we were at the gospel meeting in Tela where a fine crowd had gathered.

I am hoping this month to get out to Kilometer Siete, Agua Blanca and San Juan for Sunday meetings and, with the Lord's help, expect to be able to get out more during the next years for visits to different places.

John Ruddock
Tela, Republica De Honduras
Central America
2nd December 1947

# CHAPTER 36: Two Letters From the Mosquito Coast

Some 30 years ago, brother Alfred Hockings of Devonshire was led by the Lord to settle in the city of San Pedro Sula, Republic of Honduras, with a view to serving the Lord in the gospel. For several years he had been working as a colporteur throughout Central America and the northern republics of South America, but the need for the gospel in Honduras so impressed him that he was led to give up his work as a colporteur and devote his time to the work of the Lord in this country. Souls were saved in San Pedro Sula and an assembly was formed there. Gospel work was carried on in the villages around, in many of the banana plantations and in some places on the north coast.

In 1931, my wife and I had the privilege of joining brother Hockings and his wife. We spent almost a year with them in San Pedro Sula, and then went to live in Trujillo, a port on the north coast. It was at this place that Christopher Columbus landed at the close of the 15th century. Some of the old Spanish ruins can still be seen there, and the old cannons hold a time-honored place.

We began work in this Roman Catholic stronghold by distributing tracts from door to door, then the gospels and, where we saw interest, a New Testament. It was uphill work and not much interest was shown at first, but in time an assembly was formed as one after another got saved. Ten minutes walk down the hill from this town there is a Carib Indian village. We started work in this village in the same way as in Trujillo, and also had an open-air meeting on the beach each Lord's day. For some time my wife and I were the only two at the open air meeting, and our chief work was teaching choruses to the children. After over 3 1/2 years of this, a Carib Indian man came to see us one morning, and to tell us that he had accepted the Lord Jesus as his Savior. That was a day of rejoicing. Several other Carib Indian men professed to be saved, and the work then spread further up the coast to the Carib village of Aguan. Several were saved there and a little assembly, which goes on well to this day, was formed.

Trujillo was dependent for its existence on the work in the banana plantations which surrounded the district, and so, when in 1939-40 disease attacked the banana plants, the plantations became a failure. The fruit companies began to move the people to other parts of the country by the thousands and Trujillo lost the greater part of its inhabitants. Many of the Christians moved away, too, and we found ourselves almost where we had begun. What at first seemed to be a calamity afterward turned out to be a blessing, for wherever the believers went they testified for Christ and in many places held gospel meetings, and so the Word was spread.

Brother James Scollon and his wife joined us in 1938 and were led to settle in the port of La Ceiba, where they are carrying on a fine work for the Lord.

The question of transportation from Trujillo to the many places became a problem to us as the railroad was lifted, and our only means of getting out was by an erratic boat service or an occasional plane. We felt very much concerned about this, and after much prayer felt led to settle in Tela, where there was a small assembly, and the Christians had been pleading for help.

Tela would be an obscure, insignificant town were it not for the fact that it is one of the chief ports for the export of bananas. Each year thousands and thousands of bunches of this delicious fruit are shipped from this port. While living in Trujillo, we had often visited Tela, as also did Brother Hockings. The Christians had built a small hall (church building); the architect and builder being a dear old brother who could neither read nor write, and who, prior to his conversion, had been a great political man and was often mixed up in revolutionary activities. This hall has been enlarged twice during the past six years.

A railroad runs from Tela through the banana plantations for many miles, and all along this track are found men and women who have been saved and are now living for God. There are also some assemblies to be found along this line. Some of these

Christians were remarkable characters before God met and saved them. One man used to go around with a revolver on each hip and, when under the influence of drink, was a man to be avoided. Another, who is most active now in the gospel, had to be bound with ropes when drunk, and it was just after one of these attacks that a servant of the Lord who believed in sowing beside all waters spoke to him about his soul. Not long after this he was wonderfully saved.

Conferences are held in different places during the year, and there is always a very good attendance for the three to four days that they last. These conferences are times of real help for the believers, and are a testimony in the places in which they are held. I remember after one of the conferences at La Ceiba, when over 300 had gathered for the four days of meetings, that an unsaved person wondered how so many people could be together for so many days without having a fight. This was an opportunity for one of the brethren to tell him how God had saved their souls and made them all one in Christ.

In recent letters from brother Hockings telling us about the activities in the different places, we learned that 32 believers have been baptized since we left at the beginning of the year. This has been a joy to us and we thank the Lord for it. There have also been disappointments, and we have many times to bow in sorrow before the Lord as we see some who used to be bright wander off. We feel the Christians need more help than there is time, with the limited number of workers, to give them.

There is a ready ear for the gospel in Honduras and tracts, as a rule, are well received. When traveling on the trains, the people will often come to us and ask for booklets. Many who will not come into the halls to hear the gospel because of fear of being seen will stand outside throughout the whole meeting and listen to what is being said.

The following are extracts from a letter recently received from Mrs. Scollon, telling us about a trip she and her husband made to Trujillo and the Carib Indian village of Aguan.

"We had a nice trip to Trujillo although a short one as usual. The meetings were very good. We held them in a room in the Hode's house just across the street from the prison. As the guards wanted to come to the meeting, they brought their prisoners along with them. A few soldiers came too and a good number of others from the town. Doña Florinda hardly knows what to do with her Sunday school lately. At first it was for the children, then some women began to come and now some men are coming, and they say their verses along with the children. One is a guard at the prison and he says he is saved.

"We went on to the Carib village of Aguan and had a lovely trip. Lydia Cloter was baptized and also her sister, who was to have been baptized last year but put it off because her husband threatened to leave her. He put her out of the house one night at midnight without any clothes and beats her plenty, but she says even if he does beat her, she wanted to be baptized."

The first extract shows the need for more workers. Doña Florinda has carried on the Sunday school in Rio Cristales and Trujillo since we left there for Tela. Through lameness in her legs she was unable to go to Rio Cristales for the Sunday school, and so she solved the problem by having the children come to her house. God is using this sister in a wonderful way to spread the gospel. Seven in her own household have been saved during the past six or seven years.

In Brother Scollon's last letter to us, he stressed the fact that we need more workers in Honduras, and asked if any of the young folks seemed interested. We are praying, and we ask the Lord's people, too, to pray to the Lord of the harvest, that He will send forth laborers into His harvest. Pray too that the Lord will help those of us who are already faithful in our service for Him.

John Ruddock
Trujillo, Republica de Honduras,
Central America
4th November 1946

*Jesus himself drew near and went with them.* Luke 24:15

### WOULD YOU GO BACK?

*If you had been to foreign lands,*
*Where weary souls stretch out their hands*
*To plead, yet no one understands;*
*Would you go back? Would you?*

*If you had seen the women bear*
*Their heavy loads with none to share;*
*Had heard them weep, with none to care;*
*Would you go back? Would you?*

*If you had seen them in despair,*
*Beat their breasts, and pull their hair,*
*While demon powers filled the air;*
*Would you go back? Would you?*

*If you had walked through Honduras sand,*
*Your hand within the Saviour's hand*
*And knew He'd called you to that land;*
*Would you go back? Would you?*

*If you had seen the Christian die,*
*With ne'er a fear tho' death was nigh,*
*Had seen them smile and say goodbye,*
*Would you go back? Would you?*

*Yet still they wait, a weary throng,*
*They've waited, some so very long,*
*When shall despair be turned to song?*
*I'm going back! Would you?*

AUTHOR UNKNOWN

*Yes, I would go back. But no I can't,*
*I have gone back and back and back.*
*Now I've reached four score and ten,*
*My legs are still and painful, too,*
*My eyes are dim, my hearing gone*
*More fit for Heaven, than traveling now.*
*No, I can't go back. Can you? Can you?*

JOHN RUDDOCK

The following is from an Irish Magazine, *Harvest Fields*:

## Called Home:

**Mr. John Ruddock** (formerly of Honduras) on 21st February 1988, in California.

John Ruddock was born in Growell on 17th December 1897. He was saved at the age of 21 years and immediately joined with Ernest Wilson in witnessing for Christ and preaching the gospel as opportunities arose. In 1921, the entire Ruddock family moved to Los Angeles and John became active in work among Spanish-speaking peoples. He married Nettie Baird, a native of Scotland, in 1926 and, shortly after their wedding, they went to Guatemala to help in the work of the Lord. Six years later, they were commended by the assemblies in Los Angeles to serve the Lord in Honduras, first in San Pedro Sula, later in Trujillo and then in Tela, until their return to California in 1978.

When John and Nettie Ruddock first joined in the work in Honduras, there was probably only one assembly in the entire country. Means of communication were limited. The Ruddocks traveled where they could by train and climbed the steep mountain slopes on foot or by mule. They suffered from frequent attacks of malaria. John Ruddock labored with all the energy at his command, preached the gospel, discipled converts, taught from house to house, built meeting halls, saw assemblies formed in places that were remote, and still found time to make journeys with other brethren into the neighboring countries of Costa Rica and Nicaragua. Today, there are 160 assemblies in the Republic of Honduras. John and Nettie Ruddock are remembered with love and appreciation by thousands of believers in all parts of the republic. No words can be formed to adequately express what John and Nettie Ruddock were enabled by God to contribute to the work in Central America during 52 years of dedicated service.

When, of necessity, John and Nettie Ruddock moved to the Western Assemblies home in California in March, 1978, they were not retiring from the Lord's work. They began to collect Scripture texts in Spanish and to combine them with magazine-sized colored pictures. They sent out more than 500 per month for distribution as Sunday school prizes and in work among adults in Costa Rica, Guatemala, El Salvador and Honduras.

Most recently, having obtained a book on the history of the Ruddock family, which gave names and addresses of members in many parts of the world, John Ruddock wrote to each telling of his birthplace, childhood, immigration, marriage and work, and making clear God's way of salvation. When replies came, he sought to maintain the contact; a few were believers, but most were not. Words are not adequate, paragraphs are not adequate, an intended book will not be adequate; only the records of heaven will tell how far-reaching for God was the life of the young man who had fallen to his knees at his work place in Ireland in 1918, and cried aloud, "God be merciful to me a sinner." He may have contemporaries but where are his successors?